Twice as Much

RANDALL J. BREWER

CONTENTS

TWICE AS MUCH

INTRODUCTION

The life of the prophet Elisha stands as one of the most remarkable and faith-filled narratives in all of Scripture. Though often overshadowed by his predecessor, the fiery and bold prophet Elijah, Elisha's ministry unfolds with a quiet yet undeniable power. He was a man who lived at the intersection of heaven and earth, moving with a confidence that came not from human strength, but from a deep trust in the God of Israel. His story is a tapestry of miracles, divine encounters, and prophetic insight—woven together to reveal the steadfast love and unshakable sovereignty of the Lord.

Elisha enters the biblical record during a turbulent period in Israel's history. The northern kingdom was steeped in idolatry, political corruption, and spiritual decline. Kings rose and fell, altars to false gods polluted the land, and the covenant relationship between Yahweh and His people seemed perilously frayed. Into this dark setting, God raised up prophets as His mouthpieces—men who spoke truth to power and called the nation back to righteousness. Elijah was the first great figure of this prophetic era, confronting kings and calling down fire from heaven. But when Elijah's time came to an end, God chose Elisha to continue the mission, ensuring that His word would not be silenced.

Unlike Elijah's dramatic, solitary presence, Elisha's ministry was marked by a more relational and compassionate approach.

Where Elijah often thundered with judgment, Elisha frequently displayed the tender mercy of God. His miracles were not only grand demonstrations of divine might—such as parting the Jordan River or raising the dead—but also acts of personal care. He purified poisoned stew to save a group of prophets, multiplied a widow's oil to rescue her from debt, and healed the bitter waters of a spring so that a city might thrive. Each miracle served as a living sermon, reminding Israel that God's power was not distant or abstract, but present and personal.

From the moment he was called, Elisha demonstrated an unwavering commitment to the prophetic life. He was first introduced as a young farmer, plowing a field behind twelve yoke of oxen—a symbol of his prosperous background. Yet when Elijah cast his prophetic mantle upon him, Elisha immediately left everything behind. He slaughtered his oxen, burned his plow, and set out to follow God's call. There was no turning back. This radical act of surrender set the tone for his entire ministry, showing that true service to the Lord requires total devotion.

Elisha's story is also a profound testament to the power of spiritual succession and mentorship. Before his departure, Elijah asked what final blessing Elisha desired, and Elisha boldly requested a "double portion" of his master's spirit. This was not a plea for personal greatness, but for the spiritual capacity to fulfill the enormous task ahead. God honored that request, and Elisha's ministry would ultimately be marked by twice as many recorded miracles as Elijah's, signifying the abundant provision of God for those who dare to ask.

Throughout his life, Elisha navigated encounters with kings and commoners, warriors and widows, foreigners and Israelites. He guided armies, advised monarchs, and comforted the lowly. He witnessed both the hardness of human hearts and the relentless mercy of God. His ministry spanned decades, leaving an indelible imprint on the nation of Israel and offering timeless lessons for believers today.

To study Elisha is to be reminded that the God who parted the waters of the Jordan, who healed the leper Naaman, and who fed multitudes with a few loaves of bread is the same God who works in our lives now. His story challenges us to trust more deeply, to obey more fully, and to believe more boldly in the miraculous power of the Lord. Elisha's life is not merely an ancient record of prophetic exploits; it is an invitation to step into a living faith, where God still moves in ways beyond human understanding.

This book seeks to explore the life and ministry of Elisha in all its depth and richness. It will trace his journey from a simple farmer to a mighty prophet, examine the spiritual truths behind his miracles, and draw connections to our own walk with God. As you turn these pages, may you discover not only the story of a remarkable man of God, but also the heartbeat of a faithful and unchanging Lord who continues to call His people to lives of surrender, courage, and wonder.

| 1 |

"TWICE AS MUCH"

E lijah's time on earth and his role as a prophet of God was coming to an end so God sent him to Abel Meholah to anoint a young man named Elisha to be his successor (1 Kings 19:16). From that day forward the threefold cord of faith, miracles, and divine purpose intertwined with each other continually in the life of this young man chosen by God to be Elijah's replacement. Elisha was a great man of God and was one of the greatest prophets in the Old Testament. Next to Jesus he did more miracles than any other person in the Bible. The impact he made in the world around him will captivate your imagination. The things he did transcends all religious boundaries. His world was a world of divine purpose and profound destiny. What made him stand out was his unfathomed desire to serve God. So great was this desire that he asked for a double portion of the anointing that was on Elijah his predecessor.

He received his request and went on to perform sixteen miracles compared to the eight miracles of Elijah. He did twice as much because he received a double portion anointing. Elisha was a man who wanted to do more because he believed God wanted to do more, that He wanted to do exceedingly abundantly above all that we ask or think (Eph. 3:20). We learn from the life of Elisha that God has more for the person who wants more. We should all want more of God's presence and more of His power working in our lives. The good news is that God delights when His people want to do twice as much as anyone else. He delights when they hunger and thirst to do more for Him. As God works in you, He'll begin to work through you. As your desire to serve Him abundantly grows and grows, before long miracles will begin to happen in your life.

God desires to show Himself powerful in your life. When you walk by faith you understand that God is a powerful God who delights to show Himself powerful in the lives of His children. For several years Elisha faithfully followed and served Elijah. He observed all the great things God did through him and one day he decides he wanted God to work through him also. Not only that, but he wanted God to do twice as much as He did with Elijah. That's why he asked, "Let me inherit a double portion of your spirit" (2 Kings 2:9). We learn from the story of Elisha that God does extraordinary things through ordinary people. Elisha was a simple farmer and had no theological or prophetic background. He lived the simplicity of a rural life as he faithfully and diligently plowed the fertile fields on the family farm nestled between the rolling hills and fruitful plains of Abel Meholah.

Indeed, God's ways are different than our ways (Is. 55:8,9). He will choose a herdsman like Amos (Amos 7:14), a persecutor like Paul (Acts 9:1,2), and an uneducated man like Peter (Acts 4:13) to do His work. Paul said in 1 Cor. 1:26, "Think of what you were when you were called. Not many of you were wise by human standards; not many were influential, not many were of noble birth." Vs. 27, 28, "But God chose the foolish things of the world to shame the wise; God chose the weak things of the world to shame the strong. God chose those things despised by the world, things counted as nothing at all, and used them to bring to nothing what the world considers important." Don't fall into error thinking the heroes of the Bible were any different than you are. They weren't. They were ordinary people through whom God did extraordinary things.

God is no respecter of persons (Acts 10:34) which means what He did through them He is willing to do through you. He wants to use you to do extraordinary things. We also learn that God places special desires in the hearts of His people. He gave Elisha the desire to have a double portion of the spirit that was on Elijah. 2 Kings 2:9 (NET) says, "May I receive a double portion of the prophetic spirit that energizes you." God gave Elisha the heavenly desire to do twice as much as Elijah. Ps. 37:4 says, "Delight yourself in the Lord and He will give you the desires of your heart." When you diligently seek to please God, His desires become your desires. Jesus said in John 4:34, "My food is to do the will of Him who sent Me and bring it to completion." What you want is a reflection of God's desires in your own heart.

Don't dismiss those radical desires in your heart that seem to come from nowhere. Most likely this is God giving you the desire to do extraordinary things for Him. You need to know that God's plan for you and your life is bigger than you can imagine. His plan gets revealed to you in the form of the desires He puts in your heart. Not only does God give you the desire to fulfill His plan and purpose for your life, He also delights in turning those desires into a tangible reality. Elisha desired a double portion, and he received a double portion. God gave him the desires of his heart. Ps. 103:5 says God "satisfies your desires with good things." Jesus said in John 16:24, "Until now you have not asked for anything in My name. Ask and you can be sure that you'll receive what you ask for, and your joy will have no limits."

Elisha was a very determined and focused man. He always kept his eyes on the prize. He must have said, "It's either a double portion or nothing at all." Determination and focus are two very vital traits of the highly successful. Without them nothing worthwhile can be accomplished because certainly challenges will come. Elisha desired a double portion. He hungered for it and was determined to get it. Desire is the starting point of all accomplishment. It's like a spark that sets a big forest ablaze. Elisha knew exactly what he wanted out of his relationship with Elijah. His goal was clearly defined. He wanted a double portion of Elijah's anointing. If a person cannot clearly define what exactly they want out of life, and clearly define their purpose and goals, they'll jump on every bandwagon that comes along.

Ultimately this will lead to a life of frustration and under-achievement. Elisha was daring and dreamed big, and you need to do the same thing. Do you have the courage to dream big dreams? Do you have the boldness to ask God to allow you to do twice as much as anybody else? Elisha dared to dream big. So big were his dreams that he readily gave up all the comfort, safety, and inheritance he had in his father's house. He gave that all up and followed Elijah. He went with the wild and unpredictable option of being a servant of God who wanted twice as much. If you can think and dream big like Elisha, and take daring and bold steps of faith, there will be no limit to the things you can achieve with God by your side.

Elisha's name in Hebrew means 'God is my salvation.' "El" means 'God' and "sha" means 'to save.' His name reflects his mission to bring deliverance to God's people. Elisha's first encounter with Elijah was truly transformative. It was a moment that would forever change the trajectory of his simple, ordinary life. His story begins in 1 Kings 19:19-21 when he was called by Elijah. At the time he was plowing a field with twelve yoke of oxen which was a sign of wealth and status. Unknown to Elisha, the echoes of destiny lingered in the air as the elder prophet approached him as sweat dripped from his brow as he plowed the field. As Elijah walked up to Elisha he found him busy and working very hard. God seeks those who are busy and willing to work hard for Him. If you desire to be used by God, get busy doing whatever you can for Him.

Vs. 19 says, "Elijah came over to him and threw his mantle over him." When Elijah threw his cloak over Elisha, it symbolized the transfer of prophetic authority. There is no evidence that Elijah said anything to him. He simply threw his mantle on the young lad. For Elisha this gesture was an invitation to a divine calling. It is interesting to note that not far away was a school of prophets (2 Kings 2:3) but guided by the Holy Spirit Elijah did not go there but went to a young man plowing in a field. Elisha understood that he had been anointed do he left the oxen and ran after Elijah, saying to him, "Please, let me kiss my father and mother, and then I will follow you" (vs. 20). Elijah replied, "Go on back, but think about what I have done to you." He was telling Elisha to keep in mind the call of God and not to allow any earthly affection to obstruct his obedience.

In a dramatic gesture of total surrender, Elisha slaughtered his oxen and burned his plowing equipment to signify he was leaving his old life behind. He was burning the bridges and there was now no turning back from his prophetic call. Jesus said in Luke 9:62, "No one, after putting his hand to the plow and looking back, is fit for the kingdom of God." Paul said, "Forgetting what lies behind and reaching forward to what lies ahead, I press on toward the prize of the upward call of God in Christ Jesus" (Phil. 3:13,14). No longer a farmer, he roasted the freshly butchered meat over the blaze and fed everyone present. "Then he arose and followed Elijah and served him" (vs. 21). To follow Elijah would not be an easy life. He has many enemies, most notably the evil Queen Jezebel. The same people who hated Elijah would now hate him.

Recognize that to fulfill your heavenly purpose there will be a price to pay. You'll have to give up things dear to you, people will hate you, and life may be difficult at times. But certainly, it will be worth it. Elisha was willing to sacrifice everything for God's call. One of his prominent characteristics was loyalty. From the moment Elijah called him he demonstrated unwavering commitment. Elisha refused to leave Elijah's side and thus demonstrated a deep relational bond and a shared commitment to God's plan even though the path ahead was uncertain and difficult. Elisha was a man of great faith and determination. He followed God and Elijah without looking back. When called he sacrificed the very things that supplied his livelihood. The fear of the Lord was upon him in a mighty way, and his life and ministry demonstrated the power and glory of God. Indeed, he was determined to fulfill the purpose of God in his life.

Elisha wanted a double-portion of Elijah's anointing but first his mentor led him on a journey to four destinations that shows us what must happen first if this special anointing is to become a reality in our lives. There are no meaningless details in the Word of God. Scriptures are not put in the Word just to fill up space. No, each and every verse of scripture has great significance to our lives and so it is with Elisha's journey to a new anointing. 2 Kings 2:1 tells us that Elijah first took Elisha to Gilgal. Josh. 4:19,20 tells us that Gilgal was the first camp of Israel after crossing the Jordan River into the Promised Land. It was here at Gilgal where the manna stopped falling from heaven to feed the people. Now they had to walk by faith and not by sight. For forty years they saw the manna on the ground outside their tents but all that stopped at Gilgal. Elijah brought Elisha to Gilgal to show him that living by faith is the first step that will lead you to your full potential. When you walk by faith life gets a little more difficult. The Israelites now had to plow the ground and plant seeds if they were going to have food to eat. Faith demands work on your part because faith without works is dead.

God wants to strengthen your spiritual muscles, and this is what walking by faith does for you. Also, in the wilderness Moses was their mediator with God but at Gilgal you stop depending on others to tell you what God is saying. By faith you hear from God yourself. Next, Elijah took Elisha to Bethel (2 Kings 2:2). At Gilgal you lose what you can see and at Bethel you lose what you can feel. On your journey to a higher anointing you come to a place where the of God is no longer felt and you enter into a season of silence. It was at Bethel that Jacob met God and wrestled with Him all during the night. Often God tried to pull away but Jacob held on even tighter. What was God doing? He was trying to find out how badly Jacob wanted his blessing. God said "No!" but Jacob said "Yes!" Over and over again this happened. Gen. 32:28 tells us that Jacob struggled with God and prevailed. At Bethel you learn that if you don't wrestle with God you'll wrestle with man. If Jacob had not wrestled with God, he would have wrestled with Esau who came with an army of 400 men to kill him. Likewise, if you also want to prevail in life and come out on top then you also have to enter into a struggle with God. Like Jacob you need to grab hold onto God and not let go until you receive the full manifestation of what has been promised.

After a long night of struggling with God the heavenly agent whom Jacob held on so tightly to touched his hip and threw it out of joint. For the rest of his life Jacob walked with a limp because of his wrestling match with God. Why did this happen?

What was the reason for Jacob's limp? Let's analyze what it means to have a limp. It means that you will always need someone or something to lean on and you will also have to struggle doing what you want to do. The meaning of Jacob's limp is that if you want to walk in the blessings of God and have a higher anointing then you will have to learn to lean on Him because many struggles will come your way. Forget the idea that being blessed by God means you're on a beach somewhere drinking pineapple juice as you swing on a hammock between two palm trees. This is not reality. We are in a war. Being saved and anointed does not mean that you will live on "Easy Street." Jesus said to "count the cost" and He told Peter you could have a hundredfold return on your giving "with persecutions."

There always has been and there always will be a struggle to walk in the perfect will of God. The decision we all must make is whether or not we want to confront these struggles in order to fulfill the call of God on our lives. Contrary to what the misinformed may believe, receiving a higher anointing is not a joy ride in the park. It's a journey into a war zone where strength and endurance will be needed with each step you take. You must learn to lean on God and not the arm of the flesh. Success is not free nor is it cheap. Indeed, there is a price to pay for success. We all need to realize that success is born out of adversity. Do not let your head hang low and confess that you're walking through the valley. In Christ there are no valley experiences. Some mountains are just higher than others. At Bethel you learn to lean on God even though His presence is not felt. It is so vital that we learn this lesson because the next city Elijah took Elisha to was Jericho (2 Kings 2:4). Historians tell us that it was near Jericho that Jesus spent 40 days fasting in the wilderness.

Jesus went to Jericho alone and waiting for Him there was the devil himself. At Jericho you face your toughest battle, your biggest obstacle. The devil always shows up when the presence of God is gone from your life. At Gilgal you don't see anything. At Bethel you don't feel anything. At Jericho you experience the darkest moment of your life. Jesus met the devil in the wilderness of Jericho and so will you. The temptation will be there to cry out in anguished frustration, "My God, My God, why have You forsaken Me? Why are You so far from helping Me, and from the words of My groaning? O My God, I cry in the daytime, but You do not hear; And in the night season and am not silent" (Ps. 22:1,2). Every demon in hell will show up at Jericho and nobody will be there to help you. Like Jesus you also will be all alone but we learn from our Savior that at this critical point in our lives all we can do is follow His example and say, "It is written…" During Job's Jericho experience he confessed, "Though He slay me, yet will I trust Him" (Job 13:15). This is how we defeat the enemy at Jericho. David wrote in Ps. 34:17, "The righteous cry out, and the Lord hears, and delivers them out of all their troubles."

Great battles bring great victories. After going to Jericho Elijah then brought Elisha a short five miles to the Jordan River. It was at the Jordan that Elijah asked his protégé, "What do you want?" God also will ask you this question but not until after you have passed through Jericho. The Jordan River played a significant part in the history of Israel as well as in the earlier days of our Lord's ministry. It was a place of new beginnings. It bordered the land that was flowing with milk and honey and it was here that Joshua and Caleb began their quest to conquer the Promised Land. Jesus was baptized in the Jordan River and immediately the Holy Spirit came down like a dove and filled Him with anointed power and majesty. And it was here that Elisha asked for and received a double portion of the spirit that was upon Elijah. He received a double portion but first he had to go to Gilgal, Bethel, and Jericho and so also must you if you want to walk in a higher anointing. As you make this journey never take your eyes off of what awaits you at Jordan. It's the place where your destiny begins.

| 2 |

"DISPLAY OF POWER"

Today would be Elijah's graduation into glory. It does, however, need to be pointed out that, during the lowest point of his life, this great prophet out of desperation asked God to let him meet an early death. He begged God in 1 Kings 19:4, "It is enough! Now, Lord, take my life, for I am no better than my fathers!' God rejected this request because Elijah still had much to accomplish for the glory of God. It is a consistent truth throughout scripture that God preserves us and keeps us alive until our pre-planned destiny is fulfilled. Jesus died only after He said, "It is finished!" (John 19:30). God couldn't take Elijah home when he wanted until He raised up a young man to take his place. It was at this time that God sent him to Abel Meholah to anoint Elisha to follow in his footsteps. For several years he nurtured and trained Elisha in the way of the prophet. He poured everything he had into this young man until finally God decides he can now come home.

The time of Elijah's departure was at hand. Three times he gave the young Elisha the opportunity to walk away but each time he responded, "As the Lord lives, and as your soul lives, I will not leave you" (2 Kings 2:2,4,6). Elijah did this to test the perseverance and tenacity of purpose of Elisha. A refusal to be content with anything short of the best is needed for the attainment of the highest possibilities of experience and service. Each time Elisha refused to let the older prophet depart in solitude. He followed Elijah through Gilgal, Bethel, and Jericho and he wasn't going to leave him here at the Jordan River. He would not be absent while God was doing something amazing. God honors that kind of persistence. He wants you to keep on asking, keep on seeking, and keep on knocking (Matt. 7:7). Those who are persistent are the ones rewarded with miracles. Elisha knows the time with his mentor is short and does not want to miss a second with him before he is taken away.

At the Jordan River "Elijah took his mantle, rolled it up, and struck the water, and it was divided this way and that, so that the two of them crossed over on dry ground" (2 Kings 2:8). This miracle was carried out to show Elisha the power which the Lord might bestow on him. This act mimics Moses parting the Red Sea and the parting of the Jordan when Israel crossed over into the Promised Land. God parted the water, and He dried their path across so they would not be walking through mud and filth. This was an obstacle, and God took care of it. Notice also that Elijah is at the end of his life but even in his senior years he does great things for God. Being elderly does not mean God is finished with you. There are always great things you can do for God until He calls you home. Moses was 80 when he led the Israelites out of Egypt and Daniel was 80 when he wrote the book that bears his name.

After crossing over the Jordan River, Elijah turned to his young protege and said, "Ask! What may I do for you before I am taken away from you?" (2 Kings 2:9). Recognizing the magnitude of the moment, Elisha seized the opportunity to make a request to his mentor. He said, "Please, let a double portion of your spirit be upon me" (vs. 9). He was saying, "I want twice the power of God on my life that you have on yours." This request showed where his heart was. He didn't want fortune and fame and an easy life. No, he wanted more spiritual power. Paul once said, "Be imitators of me" (1 Cor. 11:1). Likewise, Elisha wanted to imitate Elijah but to a greater, more fruit-producing degree. He was of one mind and spirit with his master as he followed Elijah for approximately six to eight years. During that time, he saw his zeal for God and his intense earnestness.

Elijah lived his last day on earth just as he had lived his entire life. It was a life of submission and joyful obedience. Some people obey God occasionally, but Elijah obeyed God all during his life. Consider 2 Kings 2:2 when he said, "The Lord has sent me to Bethel" so he went to Bethel. In vs. 4 he said, "The Lord has sent me to Jericho" so he went to Jericho. Finally, he said in vs. 6, "For the Lord has sent me to the Jordan" so he went to the Jordan. He is ready to leave this world the way he lived in this world, walking in step with the will and purpose of God. Up until that time there had never been a man like Elijah. He raised the dead, called fire down from heaven, and revealed God's plan for a devastating drought. No wonder Elisha wanted a double portion of what his mentor had. He admired and loved Elijah and his desire was to say and do greater things than what Elijah said and did.

His desire was to be like Elijah, to be like him in the divine features of his character, to be like him in the possession of the Spirit of God, to perform miracles like he did. Elisha was not only full of admiration for Elijah, not only did he want to be like him, but he wanted to go a step further and do twice as much as his beloved mentor. This is why he asked for a double portion of his spirit. This is true ambition. This is coveting earnestly the best gifts which Paul spoke about (1 Cor. 12:31). Always be ambitious for the things of God. Have no fear of aiming too high or seeking too much. Be like Elisah and seek far more and to do twice as much as anybody else. It is not prideful to desire this but is in fact true humility. It is desiring to be all that God created you to be. It is honoring His fulness and His generosity.

Elijah realized that Elisha's request was not within his power to answer. He knew you can't give away two of something if you only have one of the same thing. He knew it is God and God alone who is well able to answer this honorable request for spiritual power from on high, so he left its fulfillment in His hands. He said to Elisha, "You have asked a hard thing. Nevertheless, if you see me when I am taken from you, it shall be so for you; but if not, it shall not be so" (vs. 10). Elijah's condition was not based on anything Elisha had to do but only depended on what he saw. Clearly this indicates that Elijah is leaving it to the Lord to answer the request. To receive his double portion Elisha had to see Elijah being taken away to heaven. He had to follow his mentor all the way to the end. He couldn't walk away midway through the journey.

Elijah was saying that for Elisha to receive a double portion anointing he had to be where God told him to be. He had to stay connected to Elijah until the very end. By not leaving Elijah's side Elisha was showing God honor for the man He had anointed, and he was showing God honor for the anointing upon the man. Vs. 11, "Then it happened, as they continued on and talked, that suddenly a chariot of fire appeared with horses of fire and separated the two of them; and Elijah went up by a whirlwind into heaven." The walking and talking ceased immediately. Elisha saw the whirlwind carry Elijah away. The mantle had been effectively passed from the heaven bound prophet to the earth-bound prophet. The transfer of power has occurred. Elijah's departure left Elisha in a state of profound realization and responsibility. Upon his shoulders was now the weight of a divine calling and the responsibility to continue the prophetic legacy.

Many religious paintings depict Elijah going into heaven in a fiery chariot. This is not accurate. 2 Kings 2:1,9 says he was taken up in a whirlwind. The purpose of the chariot of fire was to separate Elijah from Elisha. Chariots and fiery horses were symbols of God's power in battle. They were the mightiest means of warfare in ancient times. God is saying His power is far greater than any military might. Elijah was taken up in a fiery tornado, a storm with thunder and lightning. The Hebrew word for "whirlwind" is "sa'ar" which means 'rage' and refers to 'a gale, a tempest, a heavy windstorm.' God's awesome display of power to Elisha fitted him for service. Such a display is reminiscent of God revealing His power to Moses at the burning bush, thus fitting Moses for service. Vs. 12, "Now Elisha saw it, and he cried out, 'My father, my father, the chariot and its horsemen!' So he saw him no more. And he took hold of his own clothes and tore them into two pieces."

The word "father" is a title of deep respect and of spiritual authority. This exclamation appears to be an expression of grief as well as affection for Elijah and speaks of the intimacy of their relationship. Notice he calls Elijah "the chariot of Israel and its horsemen!" This was a term to describe Elijah's prophetic power which served to protect Israel in times of spiritual darkness and apostasy. Elijah is viewed by Elisha as a one-man army. When the Lord spoke through him, his prophetic word was as powerful as an army of chariots and horses. Elisha's heartbreak and sorrow is instructive because his distress did not derail him from serving the Lord. He was sad but he didn't let it debilitate him from the call on his life. It's okay to have grief but don't let it drown you and paralyze you. Elisha pressed forward and went on to walk with and serve and honor his God in a powerful way.

The supernatural power of God is now on the life of Elisha. God did His part, and it is now Elisha's responsibility to go out with this power and fulfill God's plan and purpose for his life. The truth be told, that's what the anointing is for. It can be defined as "God's presence resting upon a person so they can accomplish God's divine purpose." It is God on flesh doing what only God can do. It is God's desire for every person on earth to live a supernatural life, a life where the anointing of God is on you giving you the power to do twice as much as anybody else. Elijah had been the spiritual backbone of Israel and now it's Elisha's turn. The baton has been passed and it's time for Elisha to step out in faith and believe for God to do what only He can do. 2 Kings 2:13 says, "He also took up the mantle of Elijah that had fallen from him and went back and stood by the bank of the Jordan." This mantle was the sign that Elisha was taking over Elijah's prophetic office.

By taking up the mantle Elisha was making it clear that he had accepted the responsibilities involved as he succeeded the great prophet and continued his work. Elisha was standing alone on the bank of the Jordan River. The cloak in his hand is not just a garment but a symbol of authority and divine empowerment. What happens next will propel him to the forefront of divine service. He took the cloak "and struck the water with it and asked, 'Where is the Lord God of Elijah?' When he struck the water, it divided to the right and to the left, and he crossed over" (vs. 14). Immediately Elisha puts the mantle to work and steps out in faith, trusting the Lord for the power to do the impossible. Would the same mantle in his hands have the same miraculous effect it had in Elijah's hands? Notice that Elisha didn't wait for God to tell him what to do. With faith-filled confidence he immediately steps out in faith and strikes the water with the mantle in his hand.

More times than not, God tells those who are continually waiting on Him to get up and do something. He says, "I called you and now it's your move to act on what I told you to do." The truth be told, God doesn't want to have to tell you what to do all the time. As a grown up, mature believer you should know what needs to be done. It's time to grow up and take the initiative to get out of the boat without God telling you to do so. That's what being mature in spiritual things is all about. It's about having divine intuition to do what you know God wants you to do. Elisha saw Elijah strike the water with the mantle so now he strikes the water with the same mantle. This was truly a stunning act of faith. In your walk with God sometimes you have to pull your shoulders back, stick your chin out, and go for it. That's what happens when you have ridiculous faith.

You can do that when you have the audacity to ask God for big things. Elisha asked God for the power to do twice as much as Elijah and boldly took steps to have that desire fulfilled. He acted without God telling him to act. He struck the water, crossed over, and later went on to perform many miracles and demonstrate the power of God throughout his ministry. Too many people in God's kingdom are way too timid. Recognize that God is on the move and you've got to step forward and get in with the plan. Do something. It's your move. Dare to believe for the impossible. Smith Wigglesworth said, "If you will dare to believe God you can defy all the powers of evil. God is with the person who dares to stand upon His Word. If you don't venture out in faith, you remain ordinary as long as you live. If you dare the impossible, God will abundantly do far above all you ask or think."

The question, "Where is the Lord God of Elijah?" was not a question of doubt but more of an acknowledgement of his trust and dependence of the Lord God of Israel. When the water parted God was saying, "I am with you just as I was with Elijah." This miracle confirmed to Elisha that he had received spiritual power just like Elijah had. God is no respecter of persons. Elisha knows that what God does for one person He will do for another person if they only believe. The water parted for Elijah and now it parts for Elisha. Reaching the other side signaled the emergence of a new prophet in God's kingdom. He was a man who has willfully chosen to walk an unseen path, guided by faith, and empowered by the divine.

Charles Spurgeon said, "A great weight of responsibility had fallen on Elisha. He had to do what scarcely any other person had done before. He had to follow one who seemed to be one of a kind. The great object to be desired is God, Jehovah, Elijah's God. With Him all things flourish. Those entering on any holy work should seek for the God who was with their predecessor." Consider why Elisha said, "Where is the Lord God of Elijah?" instead of saying, "Where is the Lord God of Israel?" He said what he did because Elijah's personal relationship with the Lord made a powerful impact on his life." He had followed Elijah for many years and all that he had seen and heard caused him to want to have the same monumental walk with God that his master had, the man he looked up to as a father. By calling him "the chariot of Israel and its horsemen" he was acknowledging that Israel's true strength and protection was actually found in this man of God. They were kept afloat in his presence and through his message and intercession. As Elijah was being taken up to heaven Elisha realized this was a great loss for the people of Israel.

What Elisha was saying is that he wanted God to walk with him the same way He walked with Elijah. He needed the presence and power of God if he was going to do twice as much as his predecessor. If you are a mentor to someone, be encouraged knowing that it is indeed possible to live for Good in such a way that it will encourage others to yearn for the same type of relationship with the Lord. Heb. 13:7 (TPT) says, "Don't forget the example of your spiritual leaders who have spoken God's message to you, take a close look at how their lives ended, and then follow their walk of faith." Leaders are not called just to speak the Word of God but also to showcase through their practical day-to-day living of the blessing of faithfully serving God on a continual basis. Elisha considered all the things he saw Elijah say and do. The Hebrew word for "consider" is "anatheoreo" and it means to 'look again and again.' The idea is to view or behold attentively.

The word refers to earnest contemplation and close examination, implying a keen interest in what is observed. In other words, Elijah had Elisha's full and undivided attention each day they walked together. Leaders have been positioned to cause others to say they want the same God-focused passion, so much so that they'll want twice as much as the one who leads them. It is a high calling to influence others to have the same Christ-centered purity that you have, to have the same Christ-inspired joy that comes from serving God faithfully. Your life is to radiate that type of inspiration, to show others by example the type of life living by the Word produces. Live in such a way that the desire to imitate your way of life becomes contagious. Be like Elijah and live a life that matters. Be the type of shepherd that others want to follow. Hopefully there will be someone under your wings who will desire to do twice as much as you.

| 3 |

"MOCKING GOD'S PROPHET"

The first thing Elisha did after Elijah's departure was he boldly stepped out in faith. Not afraid of being disappointed, he parted the Jordan River and crossed over to the other side (2 Kings 2:14). Not only did God allow Elisha to part the Jordan River so he would know God was with him, He allowed it to happen so others would also know that God was with him. Watching from a distance were the sons of the prophets from Jericho. When they saw this miracle, they said amongst themselves, "The spirit of Elijah rests on Elisha" (vs. 15). When God calls you to a particular ministry, He will work on your behalf to identify that to others. You do not have to pressure people and convince them of your calling. When God's hand is on your life, those who need what you have to offer will recognize it. This is why the sons of the prophets gave recognition to Elisha as Elijah's successor.

While there were a number of prophets in Israel at this time, Elisha is the senior prophet among them all. These men "came to meet hi, and bowed to the ground before him" (vs. 15). They came and approached Elisha with initial respect, but in their hearts was an aching skepticism. They wanted to make sure Elijah was actually taken up to heaven. This doesn't make sense because in vs. 5 these same prophets had prophesied to Elisha, saying, "Do you not know that the Lord will take away your master from over you today?" Elijah was not with Elisha now so these sons of the prophets knew something has happened to him having not seen the whirlwind take him away to the glories of heaven. They said to Elisha, "There are with your servants fifty strong men, please let them go and search for your master; perhaps the Spirit of the Lord has taken him up and cast him on some mountain or into some valley" (vs. 16).

This may seem like a silly request but being miraculously transported from one place to another is not unheard of in the Bible. Consider what happened after Philip baptized a eunuch from Ethiopia. "When they came out of the water, the Spirit of the Lord snatched Philip away; and the eunuch no longer saw him but went on his way rejoicing. Meanwhile, Philip found himself at Azotus" (Acts 8:39,40). Philip was supernaturally transported from one place to another. This was clearly a sudden departure. One moment he was with the Ethiopian eunuch, and the next moment he vanished into thin air. The request these prophets now make indicates they did not see what Elisha saw. He knew their search for a body would be futile so he said to them, "You shall not send anyone" (vs. 16). Not wanting to take no for an answer "they kept urging him until they shamed him into agreeing, and he finally said, "All right, send them out" (vs. 17).

Consider all this from Elisha's perspective. He parts the Jordan River and is now filled with courage, joy, peace, boldness, and exhilaration. He had just tasted the faithfulness of God. Right after this miracle happened the first thing he encounters is the doubt and unbelief of the sons of the prophets. They brought with them a level of discouragement and despondency. Unfortunately, this is not uncommon for those who walk by faith. It is predictable that discouragement will be right around the corner when God does something wonderful in your life. Understand that discouragement is strategic. It's the devil's way of trying to make you ineffective in the kingdom of God. Don't let this make you resentful and cynical, instead allow it to make you cautious. Be cautious and aware that bad news seems to make an appearance around the time when God works mightily in your life, when He creates a testimony for you to share with others.

Needless to say, these strong men searched for three days but did not find Elijah. Elisha was still at Jericho when they returned and he asked, "Didn't I tell you not to go?" (vs. 18). Unbelief will always leave you stranded and unsatisfied. They searched and searched but found nothing. It took three days for them to realize Elisha was right all along. Searching for evidence to make sure God did what He said He would do is a futile endeavor. Elisha does a little educating to the prophets here, saying essentially, "You should have listened to me." We're not told if the prophets responded to this, if they responded at all. The men of the city, however, knew Elisha was in their midst so they came to him with a crisis the city was facing. This probably pleased Elisha to no end because those who are anointed are extremely eager to walk in their anointing. They have the courage to seize opportunities for God to work through them.

The men from the city said to Elisha, "Please notice, the situation of this city is pleasant, as my lord sees; but the water is bad, and the ground barren" (vs. 19). Jericho was a cursed city dating back to the time of Joshua (Josh. 6:26). The city laid idle for centuries until wicked King Ahab came along and rebuilt it (1 Kings 16:34). Jericho turned into a nice place to live. The climate was favorable and the site of the city was delightful. Still, all the wealth and wisdom there could not remove the plague of bitter water and barren soil. What's happening in Jericho is a stark illustration of the world we live in today. On the surface the city seemed promising and profitable but underneath it lacked substance. Jericho was a lifeless city. Looking in from the outside it looked like a pleasant place to live but in reality it was dreadful and had nothing of substance to offer anybody.

This is the illusion we see in the world today. Satan comes as an angel of light (2 Cor. 11:14) and gives people temporary enjoyment from the fleeting pleasures of sinful actions (Heb. 11:25). The Bible emphasizes that while there can be pleasure in sin, it is only for a season, ultimately leading to bitterness, destruction, and eternal pain and suffering. People perceive things with their senses. As they look around, they see a general happiness in the people. There seems to be a purpose that satisfies them as they ignore God and serve their own passions. We must approach life realizing that things are not always as they appear to be. 1 Sam. 16:7 says, "For man looks at the outward appearance, but the Lord looks at the heart." So it is that Jericho was not the city it appeared to be. Labor as they may, the people's hard toil did not bring satisfaction. The water and soil failed to give them the desires of their heart. Standing before Elisha, the men of the city hoped their hopeless situation would soon change.

Elisha could have rebuked them for rebuilding the city in the first place since it was cursed but he didn't. Instead, he saw a saw a golden opportunity for the power and anointing of God to work through him. What will soon happen in Jericho will be a miracle of hope and grace. The curse on the city will soon be reversed revealing that God's mercy triumphs over judgment. Elisha makes what seems to be an odd request. "And he said to them, 'Bring me a new bowl, and put salt in it.' So they brought it to him" (2 Kings 2:20). The prophet of God requested a new bowl that was free from contamination and that they put salt in it which is an obvious illustration of a purifying agent. The men of the city did not question this unusual request from the prophet who stood before them. It was a strange request but Elisha presented himself as a man with authority.

The men of Jericho realized that Elisha was just passing through their city, and it was commendable that they seized the opportunity to seek his help when they did. Elisha went to the spring of water and threw the salt into it, saying, "Thus says the Lord: 'I have healed this water; from it there shall be no more death or barrenness'" (vs. 21). The healing of Jericho's water freed the city from Joshua's curse. The miracle is that adding salt should have made the water even more undrinkable but here it had the opposite effect. The water became purified and it was now safe to drink. Vs. 22 says, "So the water remains healed to this day, according to the saying of Elisha which he spoke." Notice that he parted the Jordan River because he was standing on the Word of God. Here, he pours salt into the water because he heard the voice of God. There is a lesson to be learned here.

Sometimes God wants you to take what you know from the Word of God and act on it without Him telling you to do so. Other times He'll speak to your heart giving you specific instructions on what to do. Elisha said, "God said it so I'll do it no matter how strange it may seem." Imagine all the good that will happen if people would only step out in faith and do what God tells them to do. Obey God willingly and faithfully and miracles will happen. The chains of bondage will be loosed and people all over the planet will be set free and live wholesome lives. Listen to the Lord and seize the opportunities for miracles that He gives you. He'll respond to your faith and supernatural occurrence will take place all around you. Indeed, you'll do twice as much. Notice also that Elisha got the people involved in the process. They had to bring him a new bowl and put salt in it. The question is, what are you willing to do in order for God to do miracles through your life?

You need to understand that the unfruitfulness of the land around Jericho was a symptom of a deeper issue. The water was bad causing the ground to be sterile and barren. What is significant here is that Elisha approaches this problem the same way God approaches the barrenness of man. He went to the source of the problem, which was a contaminated, polluted spring. In dealing with the spring, everything the water touched would be affected. When the Lord saves a sinner, He doesn't deal with their outward actions, He deals with their heart. He purifies their heart knowing that the life of the Spirit inside of them will pump grace and mercy and godliness into every area of that individual's life, changing them from the inside out. God purifies us the same way Elisha purified the waters of Jericho. The word "purify" means 'to cause something to become clean from contamination by taking away an undesirable part.'

Titus 2:14 says Jesus "gave Himself for us to redeem us from all lawlessness and to purify for Himself a people for His own possession who are zealous for good works." What comes before a zeal for good works? A purification. Losing your zeal to serve God is a symptom of a deeper issue. Something inside of you needs to be cleansed and purified. Be like David who said, "Search me, O God, and know my heart; Try me, and know my anxieties; And see if there is any wicked way in me and lead me to the way everlasting" (Ps. 139:23,24). James 4:8 tells how the purifying process begins, "Draw near to God and He will draw near to you. Cleanse your hands, you sinners; and purify your hearts you double-minded." John Blanchard said, "There is only one view more welcome than the backside of the devil and that is the face of God." The practice of drawing near to God needs to permeate into every area of your life.

Notice that being cleansed and purified follows God drawing near to you. You can be a sinner when you draw near to God, but you can't remain that way when He draws near to you. If your heart is dry and calloused, if your life is barren and unfruitful, then draw near to God and ask Him to do a healing work inside of you so that you can do what He has called you to do. He is capable of doing that if you'll just humble yourself before Him. Sin and willful disobedience put a distance between you and God, and this is why James is calling you to pursue intimacy with God. David shows us what drawing near to God looks like in Ps. 63:1, "O God, You are my God; Early will I seek You; My soul thirsts for You; My flesh longs for You in a dry and thirsty land where there is no water." Charles Spurgeon said, "The greater our nearness to God, the less we are affected by the attractions and distractions of earth. Access into the most holy place is a great privilege and a cure for a multitude of ills."

Drawing near to God is not an isolated act, something you do once in a while. No, it is a continual action, a habitual walk. It is something you do minute by minute hour by hour, day by day. Draw near to God and stand on the promise of Ps. 145:18 that says, "The Lord is near to all who call upon Him, to all who call upon Him in truth." Draw near and God will be forever by your side. Once you draw near to God, James says to carry out a thorough moral and ethical cleansing. He knows that only the pure in heart can be allowed to enter into the presence of God's holiness (Matt. 5:8). David asks, "Who may ascend into the hill of the Lord? And who may stand in His holy place? He who has clean hands and a pure heart, who has not lifted up his soul to falsehood" (Ps. 24:3,4). English poet John Donne spoke of spiritual cleansing when he exhorted believers to "sleep with clean hands, either kept clean all day by integrity or washed clean at night by repentance."

Elisha left Jericho and began to make his way to Bethel which was the headquarters of idolatry in Israel (1 Kings 12:29). It was a place of deep spiritual darkness. At one time Bethel was a very special, spiritual place. It was at Bethel that Jacob dreamed of a stairway to heaven (Gen. 28:12). He named this place "Bethel" which means 'house of God.' Later, unfortunately, Bethel became a place of idol worship when Solomon's son Jeroboam set up golden calves to be worshipped there and in the city of Dan. Hosea later called this city Beth Aven (Hos. 4:15) which means 'house of wickedness.' The word "Aven" means 'trouble, sorrow, idolatry, wickedness, and emptiness.' When men are empty of God and His Word, they will fill their lives with vain and evil things. This leads to idolatry, which leads to iniquity, which leads to calamity.

The house of God became a house of idolatry. Through the years the city grew spiritually darker and darker. Some of the most evil, notorious people in the land resided in Bethel (1 Kings 16:34). These were the type of people who lived in this city. Among them were a group of young men who ridiculed the man of God. They were very hostile and were against God and those who served Him. "As he was going up the road, some youths came from the city and mocked him, and said to him, 'Go up, you baldhead! Go up, you baldhead!'" (2 Kings 2:23). They did not mock the prophet of God just one time, they mocked him repeatedly. Mocking God's prophet was sadly a picture of what the entire nation of Israel would often do to God's prophets. 2 Chron. 36:16 says, "They continually mocked the messengers of God, despised His words, and scoffed at His prophets, until the wrath of the Lord arose against His people, until there was no remedy."

These were young men who were mocking Elisha and not children. The Hebrew word for "youths" is the same word used to describe Isaac at age 28, Joseph at age 39, and Rehoboam at age 40. What this means is that they were old enough to be responsible for their actions. They were not young children having fun but young adults who knew what they were doing. Elisha's lack of hair was not the result of old age since he lived about fifty years after this encounter. At this time, he was a relatively young man and his baldness was in sharp contrast to Elijah's hairy appearance (2 Kings 1:8). In the Bible, hair was seen as a sign of valor and manliness, and long hair was a sign of being dedicated to God (Num. 6:5). By calling him "baldhead" they were unfairly criticizing his role as a prophet. The word "baldhead" was a term of scorn in the Old Testament. Natural baldness was very rare in those days, so scarce was baldness that it carried with it a suspicion of leprosy (Is. 3:17,24).

This was a deliberate act. They saw the prophet walking by and they came out of the city and purposefully pursued him. They began to mock him and who knows what else they had in mind. When these young men said, "Go up, baldhead!" they were saying they wanted him to leave the earth the same way

Elijah did. If he wouldn't leave, their intent was to help him do so. Clearly Elisha's life is in danger here. They wanted him gone because of their disdain and rejection of God. Those walking in darkness often respond vehemently when confronted by the light. When a man of God is rebuked, persecuted, rejected, and denied by evil heartless people, ultimately, they are doing all these things to the God he represents (Matt. 25:40). When they wanted Elisha to leave their presence, they were in fact desiring God to leave their presence as well. God took this personally and what followed next was an event never to be forgotten.

| 4 |

"DIVINE JUSTICE"

E lisha is at the very start of his ministry and right away he is facing hostilities from a crowd of young men from the evil city of Bethel who came out and mocked him repeatedly. This should come as no surprise because it is the practice of the devil to destroy you and the work you are destined to fulfill, many times before you even get started. For example, at the time of Jesus' birth, Herod had all the male children two years old and younger put to death in an attempt to kill the one born to be the King of the Jews (Matt. 2:16). Thirty years later the devil tempted Jesus in the wilderness knowing if he could get Jesus to sin it would cancel God's plan to redeem mankind from the consequences of sin (Matt. 4:1-11). Paul said in 1 Cor. 16:9, "For a great and effective door has opened to me, and there are many adversaries." For sure, Satan hates it when believers are about to step into their destiny.

God has a plan and purpose for every person on planet earth. What happens is that as the believer is about to step across the ministry threshold, right on cue the enemy attacks. It should come as no surprise that the enemy will try to steal a person's destiny. It's what he does. John 10:10 says, "The thief does not come except to steal, and to kill, and to destroy." Don't be caught off guard and think the enemy will leave you alone. He won't. Be on the offense knowing the enemy will surely attack God's purpose for your life. Determine to step through the door of opportunity with confidence in the Lord. Empty yourself of fear and doubt and ask God to fill you to overflowing with His Holy Spirit. Then rise up and run through the door God has graciously opened for you. Don't tiptoe, stagger, or hold onto the doorpost for dear life. Run through it with everything you've got.

God would not let Elisha who had been set apart unto Himself be ridiculed by these young hoodlums who had assembled together for the sole purpose of mocking the prophet of God. The word "mocked" is the Hebrew word "galas" and describes a scornful belittling of something or someone. It comes from an attitude which counts as valueless that which is really of great value. Their taunts carried a weight of disrespect and defiance toward Elisha's prophetic standing, hinting at uncertainties regarding his divine connection and prophetic proficiency. The reference to Elisha's baldness likely aimed to undermine his prestige and authority as baldness was often construed as a symbol of divine disfavor. In ridiculing Elisha's lack of hair, they were not only targeting his physical appearance but they also challenged his status as a messenger of God.

Through their mockery and disregard for Elisha, these young men not only disrespected the individual but also rejected the divine message and authority vested in him. This event illustrates a prevailing resistance among the people of that time to heed correction and guidance from God conveyed through Hid divine-appointed messengers. Confronted with this scornful mocking, Elisha did not passively endure it. Instead, he turned, observed the youths, and invoked a curse upon them in the name of the Lord. "So he turned to around and looked at them and pronounced a curse on them in the name of the Lord. And two female bears came out of the woods and mauled forty-two of the youths" (2 Kings 2:24). Not motivated by personal pride but by a desire for God's glory, Elisha has conviction in the midst of unbelief and pronounced God's curse on them for their disrespect of His prophet and Go Himself.

Cursing these young men was no random act. Elisha was fulfilling and executing the judgment of God which the people were warned about hundreds of years before this event took place. God said in Lev. 26:21,22, "If you remain hostile toward Me and refuse to listen to Me, I will send wild animals against you, and they will rob you of your children." God had previously used a lion to kill a wayward prophet (1 Kings 13:24) and here he uses two female bears to bring judgment on those who mocked Elisha and brought shame to his role as a prophet. These two large, ferocious animals became instruments of divine justice. Perhaps they thought their cubs were in danger. Without a doubt, hell has no fury like a mama bear protecting her babies. Twice these young men said, "Go up, you baldhead!" It is no coincidence that it was two female bears that came out of the woods and not one. Matt. 7:2 says, "With the measure you use, it will be measured to you."

These bears viciously mauled these young men causing most of them, if not all of them, to die a violent death. God does not take it lightly when the enemy mocks and puts His people in danger. These were wicked young men, comparable to a modern-day street gang. Hence, Elisha was endangered by their number, by the nature of their sin, and by their obvious disrespect for authority. The Bible says Elisha cursed them in the name of the Lord. A curse was a formal appeal to a higher authority to vindicate one's cause through judgment. Elisha cursed the lads, but it was God who carried it out. This appalling judgment was God's warning to all who would scorn the prophets of the Lord. He said in 1 Chron. 16:22, "Do not touch My anointed ones, and do My prophets no harm." The mauling of these young men was clearly justified for to ridicule Elisha was to ridicule God Himself. For sure, the seriousness of the crime was indicated by the seriousness of the punishment.

There is a clear contrast between the second and third miracle that Elisha performed. In Jericho the people humbly beseeched Elisha, in Bethel they viciously rejected him. In Jericho the power of God working through Elisha overcame death and brought life, in Bethel death claimed the lives of many young men. In Jericho Elisha was used to remove a symptom of a curse but in Bethel he pronounced a curse that brought a severe judgment of divine intent. This story teaches us that we are to respect the anointing that is on God's people. David could have killed King Saul but he didn't because of the anointing that was on him. Paul asks in Rom. 14:4, "Who are you to judge another's servant? To his own master he stands or falls.

Indeed, he will be made to stand, for God is able to make him stand."

TPT, "Who do you think you are to sit in judgment of someone else's household servant? His own master is the one to evaluate whether he succeeds or fails." Paul is questioning any believer's right to evaluate someone else's servant. Their opinion doesn't improve or impair that servant's position before their own master. Beware of judging others. Jesus told us never to judge people, only to love them. He said in Matt. 7:1, "Judge not, that you be not judged. For with what judgment you judge, you will be judged." James 4:11 says the same thing, "Do not speak evil of one another, brethren. He who speaks evil of a brother and judges his brother, speaks evil of the law and judges the law." The attack on these young men seems harsh but God has on occasion caused severe things to happen in order to impress upon people the seriousness of the things of God. Ananias and Sapphira are examples of this in the New Testament.

What happened to Ananias and his wife Sapphira in Acts 5:1-11 is shocking and startling and when understood it will be unsettling to a lot of people in the body of Christ. This story is a warning to people who don't take God seriously. This happens when sin is not taken seriously. This passage reminds us of who God is and the reverence he deserves. Acts 4:36,37 tells how a man sold some property and gave the money as an offering to the apostles. Acts 5:1 says, "But a certain man named Ananias, with Sapphira his wife, sold a piece of property." On the surface this appears to be an honorable thing to do. In fact, the name "Ananias" means 'Yahweh is gracious' and "Sapphira" means 'noble in character, quality, or rank.' Ananias appeared gracious and generous but he would soon find out that God is holy. Sapphira may have been noble and beautiful on the outside but on the inside, she was ugly and full of sin.

The truth be told, their names were too good for them. They went through life pretending to be something they were not. Their names proved to be as ironic as their behavior was hypocritical. An evil scheme of deception rose up in them and vs. 2 says, "And with his wife's knowledge he kept back for himself part of the proceeds and brought only a part of it and laid it as the apostle's feet." Both Ananias and Sapphira were liars and hypocrites. They were not who they appeared to be. George MacDonald said, "Half of the misery in the world comes from trying to look, instead of trying to be, what one is not." The name Jesus gave to this practice is "hypocrisy" which means 'wearing a mask; playing the actor.' It is deliberate deception, trying to make people think you are more spiritual than you really are. Hypocrisy is one of the sins God hates above all others. A hypocrite has God on his tongue and the world on his heart. A clean glove often hides a dirty hand.

There would have been no problem had they not pretended to give the entire sum from the sale. But when they pretended to give the total selling price, they proved themselves to be hypocrites. They were boasting in their gift. Apparently, they were not aware of or did not give heed to what Solomon said in Prov. 15:8, "The sacrifice of the wicked is an abomination to the Lord." The Hebrew word for "abomination" is "bdelugma"

and it means 'to emit a foul odor, to turn away from someone on account of the stench.' The root word "bdeo" means 'to
stink.' It describes a divine loathing or disgust. Sacrifices like
that of Ananias and Sapphira were foul and extremely repul-
sive and repugnant in the nostrils of God. Such is God's hatred
of hypocrisy. Not to be fooled, Peter boldly confronts Ananias
and asks, "Ananias, why has Satan filled your heart to lie to the
Holy Spirit and keep back part of the price of the land for yourself?" (vs. 3).

Notice that Satan was behind the lies and hypocrisy of Ananias
and Sapphira. He is a great counterfeiter and sought to conta-
minate and corrupt the church by causing this horrible act of
deception. The Greek word for "filled" is "pleroo" and it describes something as filled to the brim. More than that, it also
describes that which controls the one who is filled. In other
words, what fills a person is what controls that individual. In
this case, Satan filled and controlled Ananias and Sapphira. He
dominated their hearts, and this is what led them to sin. They
could have submitted to God and resisted the devil (James 4:7)
but they didn't do that. Instead, they let pride, self, the praise of
men, and the love of money possess them and fill their hearts
with deceit. Ananias pretended to give all the proceeds from
the sale to the apostles and the Holy Spirit revealed that fact to
Peter. The statement he said to Ananias proved he knew exactly what happened.

What should Ananias have done? Prov. 4:23 says, "Guard your
heart with all diligence for out of it spring the issues of life."
In other words, he shouldn't have given place to the devil. Eph.

4:27 (TPT) says, "Don't give the slanderous accuser, the devil, an opportunity to manipulate you!" Unfortunately, Ananias did just that and Peter continues speaking to him. "While it remained, was it not your own? And after it was sold, was it not in your own control? Why have you conceived this thing in your heart? You have not lied to men but to God" (vs. 4). What is Peter saying? He's conveying the message that secret sin on earth is an open scandal in heaven. This was no accident but a pre-meditated and planned out work of evil. Through this diabolical act of deception, Ananias and Sapphira were seeking to impress all who witnessed this donation. Unknown to others, this was a dishonest misrepresentation of what was really in their heart.

Jesus was always hard on hypocrisy. He said, "Beware of the leaven of the Pharisees, which is hypocrisy" (Luke 12:1). Like leaven, hypocrisy starts small and goes unnoticed. It doesn't seem to be a big deal. But if it is not quickly dealt with, it will spread like a wildfire or a deadly cancer. It deceives the person into thinking things are right between them and God when in reality the opposite is true. The leaven of hypocrisy can infect an entire church. The church at Laodicea thought all was well but God thought differently. He said, "You do not know that you are wretched and miserable and poor and blind and naked" (Rev. 3:17). Had the Holy Spirit not given Peter supernatural discernment of what was in the heart of Ananias, all would have been praising this couple for their generous gift to the apostles. It should not shock you when you see what happens next. "Then Ananias, hearing these words, fell down and breathed his last. So great fear came upon all those who heard these things" (vs. 5).

Right away, in the church's infancy, God made it plain and clear that deceit and hypocrisy were not going to be tolerated. His judgment this day helped guard the church against future pretense. Because Ananias was lusting after public praise for his false generosity, it was appropriate that his sin be exposed publicly. This is why he died at the apostle's feet. British theologian John Stott said, "It is a good general rule that secret sins should be dealt with secretly, private sins privately, and only public sins publicly." This story, along with the incident of Elisha and the angry mob who mocked him, reveal that there are severe and sometimes deadly consequences when a person acts in an irreverent way toward God and His servants. There is a warning here that people need to take the things of God seriously. Consider 1 Cor. 11:30 that says if you take Communion in an unworthy manner, you may become weak, sick, and go to an early grave.

1 John 5:16 says "there is a sin leading to death" which is willful and habitual sin. This story shows us there comes a time when God no longer allows a believer to continue in unrepentant sin. When that point is reached, God may decide to take the life of the stubbornly sinful believer. It's true, God at times will purify His church by removing those who deliberately disobey Him. For sure, "it is a fearful thing to fall into the hands of the living God" (Heb. 10:31). TPT, "It is the most terrifying thing to all to come under the judgment of the Living God." Make no mistake about it, the certainty of punishment for those who

sin willfully and habitually is assured by the Word of God. "For whatever a man sows, that he will also reap" (Gal. 6:7). And let's not forget 1 Peter 4:17, "For the time has come for judgment to begin at the house of God." Ananias found this out the hard way. A short time later his wife would find out also.

"About three hours later his wife came in, not knowing what had happened. Peter asked her, "Was this the price you and your husband received for your land?" She replied, "Yes, that was the price" (vs. 7,8). Sapphira was undoubtedly ready to receive commendation and praise from Peter for the generous gift she and her husband gave to the needy. Such is the self-deception of hypocrisy. Peter did not have to ask her this question but in doing so he was giving her the opportunity to tell the truth. Instead of coming clean she added a spoken lie to her hypocrisy. Then Peter said to her, "Why is it that you have agreed together to put the Spirit of the Lord to the test? Behold, the feet of those who have buried your husband are at the door, and they will carry you out as well" (vs. 9). Jesus said in Matt. 4:7, "It is written, 'You shall not put the Lord your God to the test.'" Testing God means seeing how far you can go in disobeying Him before He brings judgment.

Like her husband before her, Sapphira didn't have to wait very long. "Then immediately she fell down at his feet and breathed her last" (vs. 10). She was then taken outside and buried next to her husband. Not everyone who lies gets struck down immediately for their sin. So why did Ananias and Sapphira? First, their deaths were a sign, a glimpse of the future judgment for all who have the same type of heart. Second, the Holy Spirit just came down from heaven and Ananias and Sapphira saw Him do some powerful things (Acts 4:31). Because of that, the seriousness of their sin greatly increased. They traded God's grace for the praise of men. Yes, the Bible says, "The Lord is slow to anger and abounding in steadfast love" (Num. 14:18). God's patience, however, is designed to lead us to repentance, not to become bolder in our sin. Those who find God's judgment here offensive are merely revealing their ignorance of sin and God's holiness. The question to be asked is not, "Why did they die?" but rather, "Why do we remain alive?"

| 5 |

"RUNNING ON EMPTY"

Elisha is one of the most unique prophets in all the Bible. Every recorded event in his life is very interesting, very distinctive, and has much practical application for everyday life. We learn in 2 Kings 3 that God is a merciful God who helps us in the midst of trouble, even if that trouble is our own fault because of wrong choices we have made. One of the first things we learn in this chapter is that associating with the wrong people brings trouble. Jehoram, the evil son of Ahab and Jezebel, was the king of Israel (vs. 1). He decided to go to war against Mesha, the king of Moab, because he stopped giving Israel thousands of lambs and rams when King Ahab died (vs. 4,5). To Jehoram, this was an act of rebellion. He then reached out to Jehoshaphat, the king of Judah, who was a good king (2 Chron. 7:3,4). They were related by marriage and Jehoshaphat joined Ahab in his quest to defeat Moab.

Jehoshaphat should have known better than to join forces with Jehoram. Prov. 13:20 says, "He who walks with the wise grows wise, but a companion of fools suffers harm." Paul said in 2

Cor. 6:14, "Do not be unequally yoked with unbelievers. How can righteousness be a partner with wickedness? How can light live with darkness?" Light and darkness have nothing in common. They cannot coexist. Jesus said, "I am the light of the world; he that follows Me shall not walk in darkness but shall have the light of life" (John 8:12). Jehoshaphat had earlier joined Ahab in war against Syria and was nearly killed (2 Chron. 18:31). This union should not have taken place for not all alliances are mutually beneficial. Ahab was killed in this battle and the life of Jehoshaphat was miraculously spared. Jehu the prophet later confronted him, saying, "Should you help the wicked and love those who hate the Lord?" (2 Chron. 19:2).

Jehoshaphat should have learned his lesson here, but he didn't. God spared his life, rebuked him for what he did, and now he's doing the same thing with Ahab's son, Jehoram. When God corrects you, special attention needs to be given to what He says. Learn from your mistakes and don't do it again. Those who repeat their reckless foolishness do so to their own detriment and hurt. Prov. 26:11 says, "As a dog returns to his own vomit, so a fool repeats his folly." In ancient times dogs were not pampered and deeply loved like they are today. No, back then a dog was nothing more than a filthy scavenger who ran in packs and lived on garbage. Being called a "dog" was the epitome of disrespect and revulsion. William Barclay said some people "are so morally degraded by their own choices that they prefer to wallow in the depths of sin rather than to climb the heights of virtue."

He also said, "It is a dreadful warning that a man can make himself such that in the end the tentacles of sin are inextricably around him and virtue for him has lost its beauty." Helping people in need is godly but making unwise alliances with those who hate God may prove disastrous. Jehoshaphat got in trouble with Ahab as he's about to do here with Jehoram. Here in 2 Kings 3 a good king partners with a bad king and trouble soon follows. Jehoshaphat says to Jehoram, "I will go with you. I am as you are, my people are your people, my horses are your horses" (vs. 7). It should come as no surprise that these are the exact same words he said to King Ahab in 1 Kings 22:4. He is repeating the same foolish mistake. He is returning to his vomit. When you don't learn from your mistakes, when you find yourself in a circle of compromise, it will change you in a negative way. 1 Cor. 15:33 (TPT) says, "So stop fooling yourselves! Evil companions will corrupt good morals and character."

Jehoshaphat asked, "Which way shall we go up?" and Ahab answered, "By way of the wilderness of Edom" (vs. 8). Notice it was the evil King Jehoram who decided which route they should take. Edom was an area controlled by Judah and its king, Jehoshaphat. It was on the west side of the Dead Sea, and it was a wilderness area that was very dry and extremely hot. The king of Edom was going to join them in their attack of Moab. They were planning a surprise attack because the Moabites, for good reason, would not expect anybody to take this route. In contrast, 1 Kings 22:5 says that after agreeing to fight alongside King Ahab, Jehoshaphat said to him, "Please inquire for the word of the Lord today." He did not say that to

King Jehoram. He asked Jehoram what the plan was. Nobody inquired of the Lord, there is no mindfulness of God, there's no impulse to pray and seek divine direction. They were in a hurry and did not ask for God's guidance.

Prov. 12:15 says, "The way of a fool is right in his own eyes, but he who heeds counsel is wise." A fool sees no fault or wrong in who they are or what they do. Fools have the attitude and mentality that they don't need help or counsel from anyone, including God, because in their perverse way of thinking they are always right. Fools are headstrong and do what they want. Prov. 14:16 says "a fool is reckless and careless" while Prov. 18:2 says, "A fool takes no pleasure in understanding, but only in expressing his opinion." This is why Prov. 13:16 says, "A fool flaunts his folly." Prov. 15:2 says, "But the mouth of fools pours forth foolishness" and Prov. 10:14 says, "The mouth of a fool brings ruin near." Jehoshaphat listened to the foolish advice of a fool not realizing that foolish people make foolish decisions that bring trouble to those foolish enough to follow their foolish advice.

After marching for seven days, they were closing in on Moab but they found themselves in a valley "and there was no water for the army, nor for the animals that followed them" (vs. 9). This is a desperate situation. They're about to fight a formidable foe who is well hydrated and they are dehydrated. They are running on empty and are not sure they can make it. Overcome with anguish, distress, and a deep feeling of hopelessness, Jehoram cried out, asking, "What? Has the Lord called us three kings together only to hand us over to Moab?" (vs.

10). Here is how a foolish person thinks. They blame God for their dilemma when they don't seek God or say they don't believe in God. There is nothing more foolish than that. Why did Jehoram blame the Lord instead of himself or the false gods he served? Because if the Lord had led them to this valley, then he would be justified in not believing in Him in the first place.

This is the irrational way foolish people think. There is no reasoning with people like that. They think what they think and no amount of wisdom can change their mind. They were on the brink of dying when Jehoshaphat, the king of Judah, asked, "Is there no prophet of the Lord here, that we may inquire of the Lord by him" (vs. 11). One lesson you learn in life is that extreme desperation can lead a person back to God. Not just acknowledging God but pursuing God. Sometimes people need some desperate\ion in their lives. The problem with most people is they're not desperate enough. They hardly notice that the world is falling apart around them. To them it's business as usual. Life goes on anyway. God wants to stir up in the church today a divine desperation, a desperation that will cause His people to fast, to fall on their knees and pray, and to seek Him with all their heart and soul.

Jehoram is fuming as he wrongfully blames God for the mess these three kings are in. Prov. 19:3 says, "When a man's folly brings him to ruin, his heart rages against the Lord." There is one godly man among them, and his name is Jehoshaphat. He had chosen poorly and without discernment in who he aligned himself with, but he still had a heart after God. He's finding out you always pay a price when you don't put God first. Still, he loved God and knew as long as there was a God in heaven, there was no problem on earth they couldn't overcome. Prov. 3:5,6 says, "Trust in the Lord with all your heart and lean not on your own understanding. In all your ways acknowledge Him, and He shall direct your paths." Make it a habit to invite God into all the affairs of your life. Acknowledge Him in all your ways and "you will find favor and good success in the sight of God and man" (Prov. 3:4).

One of the officers of the king of Israel heard Jehoshaphat's inquiry and answered, "Elisha the son of Shaphat is here. He used to pour water on the hands of Elijah" (vs. 11). This officer's name is unknown and yet he knew the whereabouts of Elisha. The three kings were oblivious to this information, but an unknown servant of an evil king did know. This tells us that it's better to be a servant who has knowledge of God than to be a king who is clueless and ignorant and has no awareness of the things of God. Jehoram is absent-minded, but his servant is more powerful and efficient in what matters most here. He has a right understanding of God, the things of God, and the people of God. Jer. 9:23,24 says, "Let not the mighty man glory in his might, nor let the rich man glory in his riches; But let him who glories glory in this, that he understands and knows Me."

Notice that this servant described Elisha as a man who poured water on the hands of Elijah. This speaks of the humility of the prophet and that he had a servant's heart. To this officer, Elisha wasn't known for parting the Jordan River or making a contaminated spring pure. No, what stands out most is how he served Elijah. Before Elisha poured salt in the water of Jericho, he poured water on the hands of Elijah. Before God can promote anybody, He must first find humility and a willingness to serve. To do great things for God, you must first be dedicated and committed to the most menial of tasks, to things the world may regard as unimportant, as tedious and lacking in prestige. But look what happened to Elisha. He went from pouring water on Elijah's hands to healing the waters of an entire city. Now he's being sought out because three kings have no water.

Jehoshaphat responded and said, "The word of the Lord is with him." So the king of Israel and Jehoshaphat and the king of Edom went down to him (vs. 12). These three kings model for us that no matter what calamity your foolishness has led you to, there is still a place to go in spite of the self-inflicted trouble you find yourself in. Remember, these are kings. Normally they would snap their fingers and send a servant to bring the prophet to them. But they didn't do that. They humbled themselves and went to him. Kings don't go out of their way and spend their time and energy looking for people. The point is, if you're in a place you're not supposed to be, then it is required that you humble yourself. When sin and its consequences cause you to be dried up, you must be willing to humble yourself and seek God at all costs? Why? Because help from God is the greatest help you will ever receive.

What qualified Elisha to be a prophet of God? Jehoshaphat gave us the answer when he said, "The word of the Lord is with him." There is no greater qualifier than that. Elisha has a wonderful reputation. He washed the hands of Elijah and performed many miracles but the one thing that stands out the most is that the word of the Lord was with him. Strive to have a reputation like that. Yes, you are called to walk in love and do nice things for people. But more than that, let it be said that the Word of the Lord is with you. When people see your reverence for the Word, your subjection to the Word, and your adoration of the Word, it will cause them to see the blessing that comes from having a love for the Word. These three kings reasoned that if anybody could help them, surely Elisha can. What they didn't realize is not only is he an anointed prophet, he is also an honest prophet who tells it like it is.

Elisha takes one look at Jehoram, the king of Israel, and says to him, "What have I to do with you? Go to the prophets of your father and the prophets of your mother" (vs. 13). His words may seem to be a little insensitive and heartless but as a prophet of God his reprimand of the king of Israel is more gracious than what may appear on the surface. These kings are in trouble and they came to Elisha looking for help. But first, the prophet points a finger and highlights a greater issue that is contributing to the problem they are facing. The underlying problem is Jehoram's idolatry and wicked ways. He comes to Elisha because he wants help from God while at the same time he doesn't want to be devoted to God. Elisha discerns what's in the heart of Jehoram and he confronts it. Likewise, if we truly want to help people, then we must be willing to address and challenge the sins of people.

Even if people are hurting, we must be loving enough to point out to them that they are harboring in their hearts trespasses and iniquities and disobedience to the things of God. It is willful and habitual sin that causes people to be in the trouble they are in. If it goes on long enough, they will destroy themselves and their loved ones will suffer the consequences of their downfall. Elisha told Jehoram to go to the prophets of his father and the prophets of his mother. For sure, these were false and unfaithful prophets and Jeremiah tells us what they were like. Lam. 2:14, "Your prophets have seen for you false and deceptive visions. They have not exposed your iniquity to restore your fortunes but have seen for you prophesies that are false and misleading." Notice that one of the character traits of a false prophet is they refuse to uncover sin and iniquity. They refuse to acknowledge sis as sin and refuse to call people to repentance.

GWT, "They painted a good picture of you. They didn't expose your guilt in order to make things better again." This is saying that uncovering one's sin is connected to a blessing. It is obvious that there is a level of restoration that can only be realized with repentance. To refuse to confront people and call them to turn away from their sin is devastating. Jehoram was a man who needed loving and stern rebuke. He was long-standing in his rebellion because none of his prophets has the willingness and courage to openly confront him. Elisha had no such fear. He knew God was on his side so he had nothing to be afraid of (Rom. 8:31). Therefore, he was willing to have an honest, bold, and wise confrontation with Jehoram. If he didn't do that, he's come under the indictment of Jer. 6:14 against false prophets, "They have also healed the hurt of My people slightly, saying, 'Peace, peace!' when there is no peace."

Elisha makes it clear he doesn't want anything to do with an idolater. Jehoram then reminds him there are two other kings with him who will suffer great loss if they don't get his help (vs. 13). Elisha responds, "As the Lord of hosts lives, before whom I stand, were it not that I have regard for Jehoshaphat the king of Judah, I would neither look at you nor see you" (vs. 14). The prophet makes it clear that any help they will receive will be because of Jehoshaphat, a man who had made some unwise choices but was still righteous and linked to the one true God (2 Chron. 20). We learn from this that we should never underestimate the blessing of being in the company of the righteous. It is a good thing to be near those who have a deep passion for God. Joseph was a servant in Potiphar's house and Gen. 39:5 says, "The Lord blessed the Egyptian house for Joseph's sake; and the blessing of the Lord was on all that he had in the house and in the field."

Because Potiphar was in the company of the righteous, his family was blessed with health, his substance increased, he grew rich and wealthy, and he abounded with all good things. Joseph's resilience, integrity, and righteous conduct brought favor to Potiphar's household. God blesses those who honor Him and these blessings frequently overflow to others in their sphere. 1 Cor. 7:14 (TPT), "For the unbelieving husband has been made holy by his believing wife. And the unbelieving wife has been made holy by her believing husband by virtue of his or her sacred union to a believer." The Amplified Bible says the unbelieving husband and wife are "separated and withdrawn from contamination." The NLT says the Christian wife and husband "bring holiness" to their marriage. Because

"God is present in the company of the righteous" (Prov. 14:5), there is now hope for the extremely serious and urgent situation these three kings find themselves in.

| 6 |

"DIGGING DITCHES"

Jehoram had just blamed God once again for their predica-
ment (vs. 13) and Elisha didn't like that. He is staring hard at
Jehoram, the evil and rebellious son of King Ahab and Queen
Jezebel. The tension between the two of them is so thick you
could cut it with a knife. Elisha is clearly agitated and disgusted
and before he serves his purpose he needs his mind and heart
to calm down. Elisha suddenly makes an interesting request.
"'But now bring me a musician.' And it happened, when the
musician played, that the hand of the Lord came upon him" (2
Kings 3:15). To have greater focus to the task ahead, Elisha, in
his irritation, calls for the presence of a gifted musician to come
to his aid and help wash away all his inner commotions. This
is not an isolated incident of prophecy and music working together. 1 Sam. 10:5 tells how a group of prophets had several
musical instruments play while they were prophesying.

There is a spiritual marriage between the presence of music
and the effectiveness of spiritual activity. Elisha is very an-
noyed and knows before any help can be given the atmosphere

has to change. And that's what worship does. It changes the atmosphere. There can be no denying that music possesses powerful properties and its influence is undeniably spiritual. One is reminded of when David was instructed to play his harp when Saul was tormented by an evil spirit. The music was the means that brought remedy to the discomfort Saul was going through (1 Sam. 16:23). Great power goes forth from spiritual psalms by which evil spirits must depart. People who are struggling yet arrive at church late when worship is over will miss out on a big blessing from God. When worship goes forth there is no room for bitterness and wrath, sour moods and vehement outbursts. For sure, worship music will add color to the darkest moments of your life.

Elisha now has a peaceful mind and an attentive spirit. He is now ready to hear from God, which he does, proving that worship is where you hear God's voice when you're in trouble. As often is the case with God, what Elisha hears makes no sense at all to the natural mind. And he said, "Thus says the Lord: 'Make this valley full of ditches'" (vs. 16). "For thus says the Lord, 'You shall not see wind, nor shall you see rain; yet that valley shall be filled with water, so that you, your cattle, and your animals may drink'" (vs. 17). God said He would quench the thirst of these armies and their animals but first they would need to dig ditches in the valley. Why? Because faith and obedience is what brings God on the scene. These soldiers are grossly tired and very thirsty and now they're being told they have to dig ditches all day in the hot sun. This makes no sense but their lives are on the line so they must obey.

What's more, there won't be any rain nor wind to cool them off as sweat drips down their brow. They don't like it but, like most things spiritual, they must do their part before God does His part. Yes, this was an unusual word from God in an unusual situation. This was indeed a strange command because this hard, seemingly useless work of digging ditches would only make the problem worse. The point here is God doesn't call us to understand His commands; He calls us to obey His commands. To receive your miracle, you must obey God no matter how foolish it may seem. Never lose sight that you have a responsibility in the receiving of your miracle. God sees the big picture when you don't and this is why, in simple terms, you must trust and obey Him at all times. Trust that God is in control of your circumstances and somehow, someway, He will accomplish His plan and purpose for your life even when you find yourself in a dire situation.

Having to dig ditches is not what the kings wanted to hear. They wanted God to do the digging. They wanted Him to send the rain and the blessings while they only received it. Unfortunately, very rarely does God work this way. The truth is that people need to put their faith on display. They need to be busy digging ditches in preparation for God to move. When you think about it, serving God and His people is a lot like digging ditches. Christian service is often hard work and must be guided by God's revelation. What God tells you to do might seem crazy at the time but in faith you must obey and do it anyway even when your service often feels like work without reward. Don't be surprised if and when God tells you to do something ridiculous. Sometimes, if you want to see the miraculous, you will have to first do the ridiculous.

Noah was told to build a boat when it had never rained before. That's ridiculous. Joshua and the people had to march around Jericho for seven days before the walls fell. That's ridiculous. Mary was told she would have a child when she'd never been with a man. That's ridiculous. Jesus told Peter to get out of the boat and walk on water. That, too, is ridiculous. What all these events have in common is that all these ridiculous actions were things God said to do. Another thing they have in common is that God responded to their obedience. To do ridiculous things takes obedience and radical humility. You must turn aside from the reasonings of your mind and do what your heart is telling you to do. Humility is to lower yourself from where you're currently at. The armies of these three kings were on the floor of a dry valley and digging ditches would bring them lower still.

Stop standing still doing nothing. God is ready and willing to meet your greatest needs and fill your life with blessings but first you need to provide a ditch for Him to fill. Digging ditches is a sign of expectant and assured faith. It's hard work but you do it anyway "knowing that your labor is not in vain in the Lord" (1 Cor. 15:58). The Amplified Bible says you are to be "continually aware that your labor in the Lord is not futile. It is never wasted or to no purpose." Paul is saying that nothing you do for the Lord is ever useless (NLT), is ever lost or ever wasted (Phillips), is not unproductive of results (Wuest). Hang in there and keep working. Keep digging those ditches. Quitting may ease the pain for a little while but will burden you with regret for the rest of your life.

Trust God and He will reward your obedience with miracles that will maximize the work and effort you put forth. Afterward you'll be blessed beyond expectation. Notice what Elisha says next, "And this is a trivial thing in the sight of the Lord; He will also deliver the Moabites into your hand" (2 Kings 3:18). Elisha is saying there is nothing too hard for the Lord. It might not make any sense to you, but it makes perfect sense to the all-knowing, all-purposeful, all-powerful God. He is the God of the impossible. Luke 1:37 says, "For with God nothing shall be impossible." No matter what you're dealing with, the immutable character of God is that He does the impossible. Solving your dilemma is no problem for God. His great power knows no limits, and it is a trivial thing for Him to accomplish anything consistent with His holy nature and purposes.

God is a God who does "exceedingly abundantly above all that we ask or think" (Eph. 3:20). Elisha said not only would God give them water, He'll also deliver the Moabites into their hands. Notice they didn't ask for this second blessing. This is the grace and mercy of God. He rewarded their obedience by giving them more than they asked for. Elisha was saying, "You'll get double for your trouble." Keep this in mind the next time you're asked to do something ridiculous, something hard that you don't want to do. Walk in faith and obey God even though it may cause your back to hurt and put blisters on your hands. What's more, Elisha even gave them instructions on how to defeat the enemy. "Also you shall attack every fortified city and every choice city, and shall cut down every good tree, and stop up every spring of water, and ruin every good piece of land with stones" (vs. 19).

What Elisha was saying is that they were going to have a total, overwhelming victory. This story teaches us that God's supernatural provision never encourages passivity. God's grace never justifies our lack of participation. Because they obeyed God and dug ditches, they received strength through the water they drank to defeat their enemy. The bottom line is they had to do something before God did something. The lesson here is you do what you can do as you trust God to do what only He can do. This is the blueprint for how we see God move in our lives. James 2:17 says, "Thus also faith, by itself, if it does not have works is dead." TPT, "Faith that doesn't involve action is phony." The Amplified Bible says, "So also faith, if it does not have works, deeds and actions of obedience to back it up, by itself is destitute of power, inoperative, dead."

The miracle takes place in vs. 20, "Now it happened in the morning, when the grain offering was offered, that suddenly water came by way of Edom, and the land was filled with water." Notice that this miracle happened in the morning. They dug ditches all the previous day but still there was no water. They went to bed that night thirsty, waiting on God to move. The truth be told, waiting on God was probably harder than digging ditches. They did what Elisha told them to do and they are still dehydrated, tired, sore, and weary. They put action to their faith but still they are forced to wait on God. Many times this is when frustration sets in, when God doesn't move when you expect Him to move. It's times like this when you have to dig your heels into the ground and keep trusting God anyway. Be like David who said, "My times are in Your hand" (Ps. 31:15).

With God, timing is everything. This verse clearly points out that the miracle happened at the exact time when the grain offering was being offered, most likely at the temple in Jerusalem. Many offerings were given by the people of Israel at various times but Exodus 29 tells us that the grain offering was offered each and every day, once in the morning and once at night. The grain offering was given with an attitude of thanksgiving, acknowledging that every good gift comes from God (James 1:17). A one-year-old spotless lamb was also offered with this offering. It was no coincidence that this miracle happened at the exact moment when Israel's leadership was showing and exhibiting their complete and individual devotion to the Lord. The lesson here is that the greatest blessings of God are connected to our total devotion to Him. These are the blessings that are exceedingly abundantly above all that we ask or think.

As the soldiers and their animals were quenching their thirst, off in the distance the Moabites were preparing their men, both young and old, to go to war against them. 2 Kings 3:22,23 says, "Then they rose up early in the morning, and the sun was shining on the water; and the Moabites saw the water on the other side as red as blood. And they said, 'This is blood; the kings have surely struck swords and have killed one another;

now therefore, Moab, to the spoil!'" Why would the Moabites conclude what they saw on the horizon was blood when in fact it was water? In their minds, it couldn't be water because it had not rained. Back in vs. 17 the Lord said the valley would be filled with water yet "you shall not see wind, nor shall you see rain." Notice also that God did not explain at the time why this was so.

But now we know. God did not allow it to rain so that the Moabites would not perceive there was water in the valley where the three kings were camped. The sun shining on the water glistened brightly giving it a reddish glow. The Moabites saw this and concluded it was blood, reasoning that the soldiers had killed themselves. Here is an example of God working behind the scenes on behalf of the people. Just because you can't see what God is doing doesn't mean He's not working. He solved their thirst problem while at the same time he was leading the Moabites into a trap that would bring about their demise and the three kings didn't even know it. "So when they came to the camp of Israel, Israel rose up and attacked the Moabites, so that they fled before them; and they entered their land, killing the Moabites" (vs. 24).

This was an amazing victory and it happened because the people did what God told them to do. It was through faith and obedience that this battle was won. We also learn from the Moabites how dangerous it is to operate by our senses. Their senses told them it was blood they were looking at when in fact it was water. A quick analysis, followed by hasty actions, mingled with a lack of discernment, is a lethal combination. This is why the Bible says we are to walk by faith and not by sight (2 Cor. 5:7). Faith does not walk by focusing on the natural circumstances but by focusing on the supernatural Word of God. Without a doubt, the spiritual realm is more real than the natural realm. It is a very dangerous thing to walk by sight. By faith we are to look through the lens of the eternal, such supernatural vision made possible by the Spirit of God.

What did the Moabites lack in their misunderstanding of what they saw? The word of the Lord was not with them as it was with Elisha (vs. 12). Without the word of the Lord you will be deceived every time. On this day the Moabites were following the foolish proverb that says, "Seeing is believing." Walking by sight is a very childish thing to do. Any child can walk by sight, and so can any fool. Yes, walking by sight is very deceptive. The truth is the eye doesn't see anything. It is the mind that sees through the eye. The eye, therefore, must be educated so the mind will know what to properly believe. The eyes of the Moabites saw blood so their minds believed it was blood. Their minds then told their bodies to go unprepared to the camp of Israel and this brought about their death. Walking by sight says, "I believe in myself" whereas walking by faith says, "I believe in God." If you walk by sight you walk by yourself, if you walk by faith God will be with you every step of the way.

The three kings and their armies destroyed the cities of the Moabites. They stopped up all the springs of water and cut down all the good trees (2 Kings 3:25). The Moabites are surrounded and realize this is a war they will not win. In a final effort to break through to victory they attacked the king of

Edom, the weakest link among the three kings. "When the king of Moab saw that the battle was going against him, he took with him 700 swordsmen to break through, opposite the king of Edom, but they could not" (vs. 26). The Moabites are fighting to no avail but their king refuses to give up and surrender. Out of desperation he stands on a wall and performs a public act of abomination. "Then he took his eldest son who would have reigned in his place and offered him as a burnt offering upon the wall" (vs. 27). He offered his son to his false god.

This act was intended to bring favor and intervention for the god he worshipped. This highlights the extreme measures taken in the ancient world during times of warfare and unrest. King Mesha offered his eldest son to the war god Chemosh, whom 1 Kings 11:7 describes as the god of the Moabites, believing he would be granted victory over his enemies. The truth is, it almost happened as the Moabites were inspired with new courage. "And there was great indignation against Israel. So they departed from him and returned to their own land" (vs. 8). As it turns out, this was an incomplete victory for the people of Israel. The Moabites had just seen the death of their next king and their fury against Israel was great. So great was this wrath that Israel chose to fight no more. They withdrew their forces and went home with their tail between their legs. Surely this was not how they wanted this battle to end.

| 7 |

"BEHIND CLOSED DOORS"

Probably the greatest lesson we learn from the story of Elisha is that God is a God of miracles. In our lives He either works through providence, or He works through miracles. Providence is when God sovereignly coordinates the laws of nature and the decisions and behavior of people to accomplish His will and divine purpose. This is supernatural for it involves God's active involvement in the world. God is actively governing everything toward a divinely predetermined end, all for His glory. Our great God is sovereign over the universe as a whole (Ps. 103:19), the physical world (Matt. 5:45), the affairs of nations (Ps. 66:7), and human destiny (Gal. 1:5). To ensure that His purposes are fulfilled, God governs the affairs of men and works through the natural order of things. An example of divine providence is found in the story of Joseph.

The second way God works is through miracles. This is when God interrupts the natural course of events with His power for the purpose of accomplishing His will. A miracle is an extraordinary event that causes wonder and astonishment. Webster's

Dictionary says a miracle is "an extraordinary event manifesting divine intervention in human affairs." Miracles are manifestations of supernatural power that have an effect and purpose in the physical universe, and they can only be attributed to the work of God. Miracles provide evidence of God's presence and power in the world and demonstrate His authority on behalf of His people. They are performed directly by God or through one of His servants. In summary, a miracle is a divine work of God that transcends human understanding and inspires wonder, displays the greatness of God, and causes people to recognize that God is active in the world.

As we shall see, when it comes to miracles, God's desire is to partner with His people. As faith rises in your heart, you'll be able to participate with Him in the fulfillment of His will. One of the first things we learn about miracles is they always start with a problem. Something is not as it should be, and you need the miraculous power of God to change things around. 2 Kings 4:1-7 tells the story of a woman who had a serious problem. She was a widow of one of the sons of the prophets and, in her dilemma, she reached out to the prophet of God. She cried out to Elisha, "Your servant my husband is dead, and you know that your servant feared the Lord. And the creditor is coming to take my two sons to be his slaves" (vs. 1). It is made clear that Elisha knew who this unnamed husband was. He was the overseer of this band of men called the sons of the prophets, a position he inherited from Elijah.

This group of men studied the Word of God faithfully as they committed themselves to exercising and growing in their gift-ings. One of their responsibilities was to serve the leader God placed over them. This woman's husband had been a special man. He chose to serve the living God at a time when the general population had turned their backs on Him and abandoned His worthy cause. There was only a small remnant of true prophets in the land. Not too long before this story unfolds the wicked Queen Jezebel had slaughtered the majority of the prophets in her domain. This woman's late husband is to be commended because in spite of all the risks he still devoted himself to full-time ministry when the culture around him bowed down to false, blasphemous gods. The widow pointed out to Elisha that her husband had been his servant but, more than that, he was a man who feared God. A lot of people serve God but don't fear Him.

When a person fears God, they go from being careless to being careful. 2 Chron. 19:7 says, "Now then, let the fear of the Lord be upon you. Be careful what you do, for there is no injustice with the Lord our God." A man who fears God is careful with his words and mindful of his actions. He's cautious in how he interacts with others and is joyfully attentive when it comes to fulfilling his destiny. He is careful in what he says and does for he represents the King of kings and Lord of lords. He lives his life with a forever awareness of God's presence even if he is all by himself. He lives a righteous life that springs forth from a heart that is absolutely and profoundly longing to please his God. With each step he takes he says, "Not my will but Your will be done" Not much is said about this widow's husband but the very fact that he feared God is enough to tell us the type of man he was. Surely his death brought sadness to all who know him.

We're not told what caused this man to pass on to the other side of eternity. What his death does tell us is that fearing the Lord does not exempt us from the painful interruptions of life. Matt. 5:45 says it rains on the just and unjust. This tells us that both good and bad people experience the same hardships and blessings regardless of their behavior and character. Know also that just because someone is suffering even to the point of an untimely death, does not necessarily mean that such a person didn't fear God or was not a servant of God. Many people have a tendency to equate sickness and suffering exclusively with sin. As we see here that is not always the case. This man feared God and served Elisha, yet he still died. We may not always understand the ways of God, especially when it comes to the graduation of His servants into glory. All we can do is put our life in His capable hands and trust Him anyway.

The final thing we know about this man is that he was not a wealthy person. His widow is now in debt and we're not told if this came to be before her husband died or after. What is apparent is that he did not leave a generous inheritance to his wife and two sons. His family is now suffering greatly, and the widow decides to go see the prophet Elisha. Notice that this widow spoke highly of her husband. She honored his memory by saying he feared the Lord revealing she was not bitter because of the condition her life is now in. Because of this lack of resentment toward her husband one can rightfully conclude that she feared the Lord also. Because her heart was right with

God, she knew where to go for help. In the midst of her struggle, she went to the mouthpiece of God. She went to see the prophet Elisha who represented God on the earth. By faith she knew help would be forthcoming.

"So Elisha said to her, 'What shall I do for you? Tell me, what do you have in the house?' And she said, 'Your maidservant has nothing in the house but a jar of oil'" (vs. 2). Miracles start with a problem, and this widow certainly has one. Her husband is dead, and she is so poor that the only thing she can claim as her own is a small jar of oil. This is the only place in the Bible where the Hebrew word for "jar" is found. This is not a huge bucket here but rather a small flask or pouch that you can hold in the palm of your hand. "Then he said, 'Go, borrow vessels from everywhere, from all your neighbors - empty vessels; do not gather just a few'" (vs. 3). Notice he is having her participate in this matter. The prophet's instructions continue, "And when you have come in, you shall shut the door behind you and your sons; then pour it into all those vessels and set aside the full ones" (vs. 4).

Miracles often start with what you have. Many times God gives help based on where you're at and what you have. He is not interested in what you don't have, He's interested in what you do have. At the burning bush, God asked Moses, "What is that in your hand?" (Ex. 4:2). Moses has a wooden staff in his hand and God would use that rod to perform many miracles. Jesus was able to feed the multitude because a young boy had in his hand five barley loaves of bread and two small fish (John 6:9). He took what the lad gave Him and thousands were fed. Elisha was ready and anxious to help this woman in need. With a sense of urgency he said, "Tell me, what do you have in your house?" He was vastly determined to give her a helping hand. James 1:27 (AMP) says, "External religious worship that is pure and unblemished in the sight of God the Father is this: to visit and help and care for the orphans and widows in their affliction and need."

The Bible clearly teaches that widows should be pleaded for (Is. 1:17), honored (1 Tim. 5:3), helped by friends (1 Tim. 5:9), helped by the church (Acts 6:1), and visited in affliction (James 1:27). To minister to orphans and widows is to be the hands, the feet, and the heart of the Father. Ps. 68:5 says, "A father of the fatherless, and a defender of widows, is God in his holy habitation." Elisha had just helped three kings on a national stage by delivering a multitude of soldiers from a foreign army and now here he is helping a poor widow who could easily be overlooked by those around her. Never think that if your service to God is not public and does not affect the masses that it is not powerful or meaningful. Nothing could be further from the truth. In obscurity this woman had served and honored her husband and the Bible doesn't even give us her name. But here she is being given the full attention of one of the greatest prophets in all the Bible.

We learn from Elisha's instructions that God is to be trusted at all times especially when your obedience involves people who may not understand what you're doing. 1 Cor. 2:14, "But the natural man does not receive the things of the Spirit of God, for they are foolishness to him; nor can he understand them, because they are spiritually discerned." TPT, "Someone living on an entirely human level rejects the revelation of God's Spirit, as they make no sense to them. These revelations are only discovered by the illumination of the Spirit." This woman was already in debt and here she is being told to go to all her neighbors and borrow some of their possessions, specifically empty vessels. This was a call to great faith and humility. One can imagine the potential questions her neighbors may ask her or the fear of being rejected. But all that didn't matter. You can't let people's opinions keep you from obeying God.

After all, miracles require a step of faith. James 2:17 says faith without works is dead. You prove you believe God is going to help you by doing what He tells you to do. The bottom line is, if God said it, you do it. In addition to that, don't let it be a concern to you if people think you're strange or unusual. It's okay if they don't understand. Elisha was specific in his instructions to her, saying to borrow many empty vessels, not a few. This meant she had to go to a great number of people, increasing the chances of her humiliation. To her credit, she didn't care what people thought as she went forth and obeyed the prophet anyway. She didn't question if what she's being told to do was logical or made any sense. To receive from God, you have to take a step of faith even if doing so makes you look foolish in the eyes of others. The worst thing you can do is let what other people think stop you from obeying God.

Surely collecting all these empty vessels was not an easy thing to do. Just like the digging of ditches in 2 Kings 3, hard work often comes before the manifestation of your miracle. If you want to see God move, then you must be willing to move also. God's power is designed to work alongside our participation. This truth is seen throughout the entire Bible. 2 Kings 4:5 says, "So she went from him and shut the door behind her and her sons, who brought the vessels to her, and she poured it out." Notice that her obedience shines even behind closed doors. Don't overlook the fact that she shut the door behind her. This tells us that in our walk of faith we can't allow the unbelief of others to enter in if our faith is going to be strong. The great Smith Wigglesworth once said, "It is an evident fact that one man in a meeting, filled with unbelief, can make a place for the devil to have a seat."

Your faith is never going to work if you listen to the critics and all their skepticism. In life you've got to feed your faith and starve your doubts. Be willing to shut the door on unbelief. If you're going to receive from God, you can't let the distraction of doubt hinder your walk of faith. This widow shut the door because she knew that doubt dies if left unexpressed. With the door now closed, she again puts action to her faith. She began to pour the small flask of oil into the huge empty vessels. A miracle took place before her eyes as she poured and kept on pouring. "Now it came to pass, when the vessels were full, that she said to her son, 'Bring me another vessel.' And he said to her, 'There is not another vessel.' So the oil ceased" (vs. 6). This is so amazing. The riches of heaven were poured into those empty vessels because she believed the words of the prophet and had the audacity to act on what she believed.

One undeniable observation in this story about the fascinating ways of God is that He does miracles behind closed doors. He moves mightily even when the world isn't watching. And when He does move, He moves exceedingly abundantly above all that we ask or think (Eph. 3:20). Surely He provided the richest of oil just like Jesus provided the best wine at the wedding feast (John 2:10). All this was taking place while all her neighbors were off minding their own business. Nobody knew what God was doing except this small family and the prophet who told them what to do. It is exciting to know that it is not unusual for God to do special things when you are in seclusion. It honors Him when you shut the door on all distractions and give Him your full attention. Consider what Jesus said in Matt. 6:6, "But when you pray, go into your room and shut the door and pray to your Father who is in secret. And your Father who sees in secret will reward you openly."

Get alone with God and expect great things to happen. As you pour yourself into Him, He will pour Himself and all His blessings into you. This is how you live life more abundantly (John 10:10). There are great rewards waiting for you when you exercise your faith in private. If your only interaction with God is in public, you'll miss out on the best He has to offer. This widow and her two sons, in the privacy of their own home, saw the mighty hand of God move as every vessel they collected was filled to the brim with expensive oil. With no more vessels to fill, the woman looks around her home in stunned astonishment. She's mesmerized as she stares at the glistening golden oil all around her. Oh, what a mighty God we serve. One can only imagine the thoughts that were going through her mind. Surely, they were thoughts of awe, wonder, and most certainly, thanksgiving.

She had followed the prophet's instructions precisely as they were told to her and her obedience brought about this miracle. No further instructions were given so now what does she do? She does what her heart tells her to do. "Then she came and told the man of God. And he said, 'Go, sell the oil and pay your debt; and you and your sons live on the rest" (vs. 7). Notice that this verse calls Elisha "the man of God." It needs to be pointed out that no other named individual in the Bible is given the title "man of God" more than Elisha. What is your idea of a man of God? Is it a man who travels the world preaching to millions of people, a man who owns a private jet going from one conference to another? Here in this story the Bible calls a man of God one who is willing to come to the aid of a widow who could not afford her next meal or the debt she owed the creditor.

Being a man of God is not about grandeur or ranking high in social importance. It's when you discover the beauty of serving people who can't help themselves when nobody knows about it. Notice also this widow went to Elisha for further instructions. She is to be commended for this because it is easy to seek help in times of need, not so much when our vessels are full of oil. She was blessed with abundance and still she had the humility to ask the man of God what to do with it. Sad to say, many people when they become rich forget God even exists. Not this woman. She was in need, and she sought God. Her need is now met, and she still seeks God. She is just as eager to know what to do in her prosperity as she was in her poverty. May her life be an inspiration to all of us. Let us all seek God and divine direction even when there is no lack in our life. Nothing brings God honor more than that.

| 8 |

"HEART OF GOLD"

In the study of God's Word, it is a good habit to understand the history and significance of where certain events took place. As any successful realtor will tell you, "Location is everything." 2 Kings 4:8 says, "One day Elisha went to Shunem, where a wealthy woman lived, who urged him to eat some food. So whenever he passed that way, he would turn in there to eat food." Shunem was a small village given to the tribe of Isaachar, the ninth son of Jacob (Josh. 19:18). It was located three miles north of the Jezreel Valley and south of Mt. Gilboa. The Philistines camped at Shunem in preparation for battle against King Saul. This led Saul to occupy My. Gilboa which was opposite Shumen, and it was here that he met his death. Shunem was also the hometown of Abishag (1 Kings 1:3), a young woman who cared for David in his old age. Later, David's son Adonijab tried unsuccessfully to marry her.

The location of this season of Elisha's life is incredibly important because of the background of where he went. One must go back to Gen. 49 and see what Jacob prophesied over this land. Before he died, Jacob prophesied over his twelve sons concerning their lives and the destiny of their descendants. To his ninth son he said, "Isaachar is a shining donkey, crouching between the sheepfolds" (vs. 14). He continued, "He saw that a resting place was good, and that the land was pleasant, so he bowed his shoulder to bear, and became a servant at forced labor" (vs. 15). Jacob and his sons are still in Egypt and he's telling Isaachar that when his descendants enter the Promised Land they will find a good resting place, a piece of land that was pleasant. This property was the village of Shunem and those who lived there were an industrious people. They were diligent to work, willing to embrace the burden of cultivating the rich soil.

The Bible tells us that many strong warriors rose up from the tribe of Isaachar, men who during times of oppression and war did not hesitate to come to the aid of the people. Not only did they carry their own burdens, but they were also willing to carry the burdens of others. This was the background of the people and the land where Elisha now finds himself. Interestingly, the Hebrew name "Shunem" means 'double resting place.' It literally means 'to be undisturbed.' It denotes being double comfortable, double relaxed, and double at ease. Shunem was a pleasant and tranquil city. It was a picturesque and charming village and in his frequent travels Elisha would often pass through this quaint, small town. The city of Shunem will offer something to Elisha through a person who had the gift of hospitality, a person who cared greatly for his well-being and his calling from on high.

He is about to have an encounter with a woman who was not distracted by the rich opportunities of the land but instead made the most important investment you can make in this life. This investment was a spiritual one and she would show that she was a hard-working servant, not to get rich off the land, but rather to advance the purposes of God. 2 Kings 4:8 tells us she was a wealthy, notable woman who did not do what material fortune often does to people. She did not let wealth cause her to become spiritually deficient. She did not spend her money to fulfill fleshly lusts but instead was eager to serve others. So strong was this desire that she was forever looking for opportunities to do so. Then the day came when the man of God came to town, and she used her resources to contribute to the cause of God. Holding nothing back, she strongly persuaded Elisha to enter her home and eat some food.

Hospitality is a virtue that is both commended and commanded throughout the Bible. Paul said in Rom. 12:13, "Contribute to the needs of the saints and seek to show hospitality." The Passion Translation says, "Take a constant interest in the needs of God's beloved people and respond by helping them. And eagerly welcome people as guests into your home." Hospitality can be defined as "the quality of receiving and treating guests and strangers in a warm, friendly, and generous way." In Greek the word means 'love of strangers.' Scottish theologian William Barclay said, "A home can never be happy when it is selfish. Christianity is the religion of the open hand, the open heart, and the open door." Have an "open door" policy at your home so that strangers and friends feel welcome and edified. Is. 64:11 says, "Your gates shall be open continually; They will not be closed day or night."

Minister Thomas Fuller said in the 17th century, "Hospitality is threefold: for one's family, this of necessity; for strangers, this of courtesy; for the poor, this is charity." Eph. 2:10 says all believers are God's workmanship created in Christ Jesus to do good works." We display God's love when we open our door and show kindness to the less fortunate. God is honored when we are hospitable to the needy. Jesus said, "When you give a banquet, invite the poor, the crippled, the lame, the blind, and you will be blessed" (Luke 14:13). Always be ready to open the door of your home to show hospitality to others. This should be done willingly for 1 Peter 4:9 says, "Be hospitable to one another without grumbling or complaint." By serving others you serve Christ. He said in Matt. 25:35, "For I was hungry, and you gave Me food; I was thirsty, and you gave Me drink; I was a stranger, and you took Me in."

This Shumannite woman was anxious to open her door to the prophet Elisha. She wasn't reluctant to do this and nobody had to coerce her to be hospitable to the man of God. A golden opportunity was before her and she grabbed onto it with all her heart and soul. Love poured out of her as she warmly went to Elisha and invited him into her home. The Bible says she "constrained him to eat some food" (vs. 8). It appears Elisha was at first hesitant but this woman stubbornly refused to take "no" for an answer. Elisha was highly impressed with the love and kindness shown him by this woman. So comfortable was he that from then on whenever he was in the area he would eat at her home. Truly this woman used her wealth wisely. 1 Tim. 6:18 (TPT) says, "Remind the wealthy to be rich in remarkable works of extravagant generosity, willing to share with others."

God makes people wealthy to advance His kingdom on earth. If you give little or nothing to the work of God but spend large sums on personal gratification, it is time to examine your values. Matt. 6:21 says, "For where your treasure is, there your heart will be also." Jesus is saying if you put your money in the right place, your heart will then be in the right place. Charles Spurgeon said, "It is sure to be so: your heart will follow your treasure. Send it away therefore to the everlasting hills, lay up treasure in that blessed land before you go there yourself. The heart must and will go in the direction of that which we count precious. The whole man will be transformed into the likeness of that for which he lives. Where we place our treasures our thoughts will naturally fly. It will be wise to let all that we have act as magnets to draw us in the right direction."

Those people who have a heart of gold believe "it is more blessed to give than to receive" (Acts 20:35). This is true because giving is the most God-like thing you can do. So anxious was this woman to bless the man of God that giving him food to eat was not enough. No, she wanted to heap upon this prophet blessing upon blessing upon blessing. In this woman's heart was the posture of servitude. In her wealth she didn't allow her ego to be inflated. Her devotion to God caused her to remain sensitive to the needs of others. Spiritual leaders and faithful men of God were a rarity in Israel at this time. So overwhelmed was she that a genuine holy man of God was in her presence that she just couldn't sit still. She wanted to do what she could to strengthen, help, and come alongside this man of God. She had plenty of resources to do so and then one day an idea came to her head.

"And she said to her husband, 'Look now, I know that this is a holy man of God, who passes by us regularly. Please, let us make a small room on the wall'" (vs. 9.10). This woman was not only wealthy with worldly possessions, she was also wealthy with wisdom. She was wealthy where it matters most for, she was able to discern that Elisha was a holy man of God. She possessed discretion and prudence for she was able to process his character and sincerity of faith. So convinced was she of his holiness that she petitioned her husband to have a room built for him. By going to her husband first, she was honoring his authority in the home. She wasn't going to do something without his approval, and this makes her an even more remarkable woman. She went on, saying, "'And let us put a bed for him there, and a table and a chair, and a lampstand; so it will be, whenever he comes to us, he can turn in there" (vs. 10).

Make it your aim in life to honor and support the true men and women of God. Do what you can to add fuel to their fire, to help them fulfill their heavenly calling. Pray and ask God to show you ways that you can help build up those godly servants who are building up the kingdom of God. Be a blessing to them just as they are a blessing to others. Men of God need to be alone with God and this Shunammite woman and her husband provided Elisha with such a place. They provided him with food and an upper room for rest and solitude. 2 Kings 4:11 says,

"And it happened one day that he came there, and he turned in to the upper room and lay down there." He was truly grateful for what this couple had done. So much so that "he said to Gehazi his servant, 'Call this Shunammite woman.' When he called her, she stood before him" (vs. 12). She stood attentively ready to serve again if called upon.

Elisha looks around the room and sees all the effort that went into its construction. In his gratitude he wants to do something meaningful for this dear woman but doesn't know what to do. He told Gehazi to ask her, 'Look, you have been concerned for us with all this care. What can I do for you? Do you want me to speak on your behalf to the king or the commander of the army?" (vs.13). Elisha had some influence with the royalty of the land, and he reasoned that they could somehow do something to benefit this gracious woman. Her response was not what he expected. She answered, "I dwell among my own people" (vs. 13). Her response reveals another jewel in the crown of her faith. She is saying she is very content and happy right where she's at. She doesn't need an audience with the king or anyone else for she is completely satisfied with her walk with God. She finds her true joy in serving God and those called by Him.

Nothing can make you feel more fulfilled than savoring the knowledge of God and serving Him and His people. Nothing comes close to that for it is the greatest thrill you can ever have. Here is a wealthy woman who proves that. Her joy and fulfillment were not in her abundance of riches but in being a blessing to others. She served without the expectation of re-

ceiving anything back in return. True greatness in the kingdom of God is to serve Him with all your heart, mind, soul,
and strength in the place where He puts you. And if He should
promote you, and He probably will, then humbly receive it. For
sure, God is the ultimate source of promotion. Ps. 75:6,7 says,
"For exaltation comes neither from the east nor from the west
nor from the south. But God is the Judge. He puts down one
and exalts another." This woman found her delight in serving the man of God fully and completely. Being paid back for
her generosity was nowhere in her thinking. This made Elisha
want to bless her even more.

Notice how Elisha found out what he can do for her. "So he
said, 'What then is to be done for her?' And Gehazi answered,
'Actually, she has no son, for her husband is old'" (vs. 14). It
was Gehazi that found the answer Elisha was looking for. He
perceived a need that she had as he observed the situation she
and her husband were in. Deep in her heart was the desire
for a son. In biblical times it was considered a curse if you
had no children. This was a burden she carried inside of her
even though it was never revealed by her behavior and appearance. Saying nothing bad about Elisha but even he was not
aware of this inner burden. It was Gehazi that revealed this
to him proving that we sometimes need others to help us see
things more clearly. Men need to put their pride down realizing that no man is an island unto himself. Even prophets
anointed by God can benefit from the presence and partnership
of other believers.

"And he said, 'Call her.' When he had called her, she stood in the doorway. Then he said, 'About this time next year, you shall embrace a son'" (vs. 15,16). Elisha was known for performing miracles and delivering messages of hope and encouragement. His promise to her came with purpose, highlighting the importance of family and the joy it brings. Commentator Matthew Henry said, "The Lord sees the secret which is suppressed in obedience to His will, and He will hear the prayers of His servants on behalf of their benefactors." This woman appears to be in a hopeless situation and understandably this news came as a shock to her. She replied, "No, my lord. Man of God, do not lie to your maidservant!" (vs. 16). She wasn't accusing Elisha of being a liar, of course. It's just that the blessing promised was so great, and appeared so unlikely to be fulfilled, that she implores him not to raise false expectations.

So strong was her desire for a son that she protected herself from the delusion of vain hope. Her initial response is similar to the reaction of Sarah and Abraham regarding the birth of Isaac. This passage emphasizes the theme of divine intervention of the miraculous nature of God's promises. The same miracle that would be granted her was the same which Sarah received in her old age. This promise is a reminder that with God all things are possible, that He can bring unexpected blessings when we least expect them. Our responsibility is to trust Him to fulfill what He has promised. John Piper said, "Sometimes God puts desires in our hearts that seem impossible. But trust in His timing and His power to bring those desires to fruition." Do that and your hope will not be in vain. This story encourages us to recognize that God not only knows our desires but also has an incredible plan for our lives if we will only remain patient and faithful.

This woman did not seek a reward but she got one anyway. "And the woman conceived and bore a son when the appointed time had come, of which Elisha had told her" (vs. 17). The promise of a child was unique to her yet the principle for receiving a reward for services rendered to fulfill the purposes of God in the way He calls you to is not unique. Jesus said in Matt. 10:41,42, "Whoever receives a prophet because he is God's messenger will be given the same reward as a prophet. And whoever welcomes a righteous man shall receive a righteous man's reward. And whoever gives one of these little ones only a cup of cold water in the name of a disciple, assuredly, I say to you, he shall by no means lose his reward." Giving a servant of God a cup of cold water is one of the easiest things you can do. Anybody can do that, and it only takes a few seconds. Jesus said even a small act such as this will bring you a reward.

Just giving a cup of water to one of God's servants is significant in the eyes of God He is deeply touched for you are reaching out and ministering to someone who is very dear to Him. Notice that He calls His messengers "little ones" which is a term of endearment. Anything that is given to such a servant is regarded by God as a gift given unto Himself. The gift may be as inexpensive as a cup of water but it's not the size of the gift that matters, it's the motive. If you give because someone is a disciple, the reward will be forthcoming. This Shunammite woman did much more than give a cup of water to the prophet Elisha. So abundant was her giving to this man that she received the greatest reward of all, a newborn son. As this story will soon unfold, tragedy will come knocking on the door of this woman and her small child. Her faith will be put to the test, a test she will pass with flying colors.

| 9 |

"IT IS WELL"

Hebrews 11 is a chapter well known to all believers. In this chapter we are given a concise definition of faith and along with that several examples of what faith looks like. Listed for us are notable people in biblical history who demonstrated in their respective ways what trust in God truly looks like. Sixteen names of specific people are given here. Fourteen of these names are men, two are women. Interestingly, the stories of eight of these people, seven men and one woman, are found exclusively in the book of Genesis. As you advance in your reading of Hebrews 11, you'll notice that the author no longer lists specific names but instead describes different exploits of faith in a more general manner. Notice one such example found in Heb. 11:35, "Women received their dead raised to life again." Two of the most notable instances of this is found in the lives of Elijah and Elisha.

The first is found in 1 Kings 17:17-24 when Elijan raised back to life the son of the widow in Zaraphath. The second instance, performed by Elisha, is found in 2 Kings 4:18-37. No matter who you are, God will honor your faith even to the point where loved ones are raised from the dead by an explosive manifestation of God's awesome, mighty power. It should come as no surprise to you that such a miracle is available to those who believe. Acts 26:8 asks, "Why should it be thought incredible by you that God raises the dead?" Even Jesus said in Matt. 10:8 that we are to "heal the sick, cleanse the leper, raise the dead, cast out demons. You received without paying, now give without being paid." Since we're told specifically to raise the dead, shouldn't we be seeing more of that in the world today? Rom. 4:17 talks about "God who brings the dead back to life and who creates new things out of nothing."

The Shunammite woman in 2 Kings 4 loved God exceedingly proven by her service to Elisha. She was strong in faith and her story will challenge how you view the impossibilities of life. Because of her faithful service to the man of God she was blessed with a son a year later. She was overwhelmed with joy, and all was going well until a few years later tragedy struck. "So the child grew. Now it happened one day that he went out to his father, to the reapers. And he said to his father, 'My head hurts, my head hurts!' So he said to a servant, 'Carry him to his mother.' When he had taken him and brought him to his mother, he sat on her knees until noon, and then died" (vs. 19-21). Yes, bad things do happen to good people. Look what happened to Job. He was a blameless and upright man who feared God (Job 1:8) yet he lost everything he had.

For sure, there is nothing more horrific than the loss of a child. But when you have hope for the unimaginable, in this case the raising up of the dead, your faith will be strong in the God of the impossible. This devastating and untimely catastrophe happened during the harvest season for the child's father was out among the reapers. Everyone was working hard during this busy and hectic time of year. It was also a time of great joy as the planters are now reaping the bounty from all their labor. Scripture often associates harvest season with great jubilance. It was a time when the people of God would gather together and have a great feast as they fellow-shipped with one another and reflected on the favor and faithfulness of God. As the people celebrated, their joy was at its peak and it was during this time of glee and exuberance that the son of the Shunammite woman got ill and died.

There are some trials that are easy to deal with where you go on happily with the life you are living. Then there are those trials that disrupt your life in a tragic, serious way. This is one of those times. All of a sudden, without warning, this woman's dream turned into a nightmare. She must have thought of the day she pleaded with Elisha to not get her hopes up. What's needed now is faith during the unthinkable. This woman knows that now is not the time to panic, to mourn and feel sorry for herself, to ask the age-old question, "Why, God, why?" The best way to be prepared for the disruptions of life is to always stay close to God, to abide in Him always. Do that and you'll be able to draw from Him the strength and wisdom you need. This Shunammite woman was not going to let this trial sabotage her faith and vandalize her witness. It is now time for action for surely "faith without works is dead" (James 2:17).

"And she went up and laid him on the bed of the man of God, shut the door upon him, and went out" (vs. 22). In the natural this makes no sense, but these are the actions of a woman walking by faith. "Then she called to her husband and said, 'Please send me one of the young men and one of the donkeys, that I may run to the man of God, and come back' So he said, 'Why are you going to him today? It is neither the New Moon festival or the Sabbath.' And she said, 'It is well'" (vs. 22,23). The NLT says, "It will be all right." Notice she did not say, "He is all right" because her belief in God was not a denial of her present situation. She said instead, "It will be all right" proclaiming what she believed would happen. This was her statement of faith. This is what she based her actions on. She is doing what Rom. 4:17 tells all of us to do, to "call those things which be not as though they were."

What stands out most about this woman is her composure. Her son had just died in her arms, yet she is rich in faith and understood this child was miraculously provided by God. She never lost sight of the origin of this story. She did not sulk and say, "The Lord giveth, the Lord taketh away." She was convinced in her heart that God did not lose control of His sovereignty. She is refusing to let her current pain be the link to her future. What keeps a lot of people from believing God at times like this is they let their pain become bigger than the promise of God. God has big plans for your future. There is a promise of God for your life, on your life, and even for the pain in your life. This woman chose to believe that in spite of what she's now facing. To receive your miracle, you must not focus on your pain but on the God who made you a promise. 2 Cor. 1:20

says, "For all the promises of God are in Him Yes, and in Him Amen."

Choose to believe God in spite of everything that is happening to you. Confess out loud that He is your hope and your salvation. Don't let anyone or anything convince you otherwise. David knew God can be trusted. Ps. 62:5-8 says, "Yes, my soul, find rest in God; my hope comes from Him. Truly He is my rock and my salvation; He is my fortress; I will not be shaken. My salvation and my honor depend on God; He is my mighty rock, my refuge. Trust in Him at all times, you people; pour out your hearts to Him, for God is our refuge." When do you trust in God? At all times, especially when your world has caved in around you. Be like the Shunammite woman who said, "It is well. It will be all right." Notice also that she didn't tell her husband their son had died. She didn't want to hear him tell her to start planning for a funeral. Surround yourself with people who will believe with you and not against you.

Because she knew God was behind the birth of this child, she also knew He was in control of his destiny as well. He would not give her a son only to have her lose him a few short years later. This is not to say she did not feel grief. Vs. 27 said "her soul is in deep distress." Having faith doesn't mean you won't have emotions. It does, however, cause you to remain grounded in what you're believing for. Hope in God is called "an anchor of the soul" (Heb. 6:19) and provides stability and security in our lives. This hope is "both sure and steadfast" and gives you a strong foundation to stand on. This anchor will not let the promises of God be carried away in the midst of the storm. It was her faith and hope that caused this woman to seek intervention from the man of God. Vs. 24,25 says, "Then she saddled a donkey, and said to her servant, 'Drive, and go forward; do not slacken the pace for me unless I tell you.' So, she departed and went to the man of God at Mount Carmel.

This was a five-hour journey in a desert heat that was almost unbearable. But she pressed on anyway. Nothing was going to stop her from getting to the man of God. "And so it was, when the man of God saw her afar off, that he said to his servant Gehazi, 'Look, there is the Shunammite woman'" (vs. 25). Apparently, he sensed something was wrong. "Please run now to meet her, and say to her, 'Is it well with you? Is it well with your husband? Is it well with the child?' And she said, 'It is well'" (vs. 26). The Hebrew word for "it is well" is "Shalom" which means 'peace; to be full of well-being.' It is derived from the root word "Shalem" which means 'to be complete or whole.' In Is. 9:6, Jesus is called the "Prince of Peace." Paul goes on to say in 2 Thess. 3:16, "Now may the Lord of peace Himself give you peace at all times and in every way."

Notice that the Shunammite woman said nothing more to Gehazi other than "it is well." Perhaps she didn't want to be detained. Time was of the essence and she had to get to the man of God as quickly as possible. Or perhaps there was another reason. Could it be that this perceptive, discerning woman sensed a character flaw in Gehazi that made her uncomfortable talking to him? Look what happens next. "Now when she came to the man of God at the hill, she caught him by the feet, but Gehazi came near to push her away" (vs. 27). That's not how you treat a woman in distress. Elisha rebuked him for it, saying, "Leave her alone, for her soul is in deep distress, and the Lord has hidden it from me, and has not told me" (vs. 27). Gehazi was insensitive, lacking tenderness and patience for others. He did not demonstrate the same love and compassion for people that Elisha did throughout his ministry.

It is no wonder that Elisha is called " the man of God" more times than any other person in the Bible. He personified what walking in love is all about for he helped people wherever he went. Paul told the saints in Philippi, "I have you in my heart" (Phil. 1:7). This is a wonderful model for ministry for this is what a man of God does, he puts people in his heart. If you want to have a wonderful ministry, if you want to be effective as a man of God with no shortage of opportunities to help people, you must first let them know you love them. Use your words and actions to convince others that you really do care about them. Let them perceive that you want to see them blessed in every area of their life. Elisha had this Shunammite woman and her family in his heart and he cared greatly about the distress she was now in. In no way was he going to let Gehazi stop him from ministering to her.

Elisha's humility is to be commended. Here is one of the most reputable and well-regarded prophets in all redemptive history openly admitting there are things the Lord didn't tell him. He didn't pretend to know everything. The Lord didn't tell him why this woman was grieving and it is refreshing that he would admit that. This reveals the strength of his character. He was not foretold that this tragedy would happen and he's now left standing in the dark. Many times, this is when we receive direction from above, when we don't know what's going on. Not only is this woman's faith being tested, so also is the faith of Elisha. True faith is tested faith that leans upon the mighty arm of God when we don't have all the answers. Consider Is. 50:10, "Who among you fears the Lord and obeys the voice of His Servant? Let him who walks in darkness and has no light trust in the name of the Lord and rely on his God."

This verse was written to godly people, to those who fear God and obey the voice of the Lord. It's saying there will be times when you'll have no sense of direction or clarity on the matter at hand. There will be times when you won't know what to do or where to go. No one is exempt from experiences like this. You are, however, commanded to trust in and rely on the Name of the Lord. God had turned the light of revelation off and as Elisha stood there looking at this woman in deep distress, he knows the only thing he can do is trust God. The grieving woman now speaks. "She fell to the ground before him and caught hold of his feet. Then she said, 'Did I ask you for a son, my lord? And didn't I say, "Don't deceive me and get my hopes up"?'" (vs. 27,28). These are the words of a grief-stricken mother dealing with the tragedy of losing her only child. These are raw emotions and she's saying she'd rather had been left childless than to have one and have it taken away.

This is a woman of great faith do don't mistake her pain for unbelief. If she didn't believe God can raise the dead, then she wouldn't have come to the prophet in the first place. She proved how strong her faith was by laying her son's body on the bed of the prophet instead of burying him. She voiced her faith when she told her husband everything would be all right. She knows in her heart that God is the God of the turn-around. She knows that when you've had a setback, you don't take a step back, you get ready for a comeback. Resurrection always starts from a dead-end. She knows that God can make a dead heart start beating again. This is why she saddled her donkey and traveled to the man of God. Without responding to her, Elisha said to Gehazi, "Get ready to travel; take my staff and go! Don't talk to anyone along the way. Go quickly and lay the staff on the child's face" (vs. 29).

Elisha sent Gehazi ahead of him because he was younger and could get to the child more speedily. The woman chose to stay with Elisha and together they set off to where the child lay (vs. 30). "Gehazi hurried on ahead and laid the staff on the child's face, but nothing happened. There was no sign of life. He returned to meet Elisha and told him, 'The child is still dead'" (vs. 31). Gehazi served the most powerful spiritual leader of his day and yet he's nothing more than a spectator in terms of God's activity and God's power. He's on the sidelines watching things unfold. He's completely ineffective here. He's seen several miracles already and he'll see more but they haven't moved his heart to the point where faith rises up in him on a personal level. The reason God does miracles is always to bring Himself glory and to build up our faith. Why? Because He'll put you in the paths of people who need to know that He is a miracle-working God.

"And when Elisha came into the house, there was the child, lying dead in the bed. He went in therefore, shut the door behind the two of them, and prayed to the Lord" (vs. 32,33). He was not going to let the failure of Gehazi deter him. Where Gehazi saw a dead-end, Elisha saw the potential for a resurrection. So, what did he do? He prayed to the God who raises the dead. Never underestimate the power of private prayer. James 5:16 says, "The effectual fervent prayer of a righteous man avails much." Elisha prayed and then took action like all men of faith do. "And he went up and lay on the child, and put his mouth on his mouth, his eyes on his eyes, and his hands on his hands; and he stretched himself out on the child, and the flesh of the child became warm. Elisha got up, walked back and forth across the room once, and then stretched himself out again on the child. This time the boy sneezed seven times and opened his eyes" (vs. 34,35).

What caused this miracle to happen? Prayer! Elisha was a seasoned prophet who never forgot that true success in ministry is prayer for this is what releases the power of God. "And he called Gehazi and said, 'Call this Shunammite woman.' So he called her. And when she came in to him, he said, 'Pick up your son.' So she went in, fell at his feet and bowed before him, overwhelmed with gratitude. Then she took her son in her arms and carried him downstairs" (Vs. 36,37). This story shows the resurrection power of God at work. It also shows how faith perseveres in prayer. At first the boy became worm but had not yet awaken from the dead. Elisha did not quit like Gehazi did. No, he pressed in and seized the moment by faith.

He did not quit until he saw the results he was praying for. For sure, the boy's mother was grateful he did.

| 10 |

"A SPIRITUAL FEAST"

There should be no doubt in your mind that God is a God of provision. Phil. 4:19 says, "And my God shall supply all your need according to His riches in glory in Christ Jesus." The Passion Translation says, "I am convinced that my God will fully satisfy every need you have, for I have seen the abundant riches of glory revealed to me through Jesus Christ!" As 2 Kings 4 comes to a close, there are two brief accounts where miracles of supernatural provision take place. Vs. 39 says, "And Elisha returned to Gilgal, and there was a famine in the land." One characteristic of a severe famine is a shortage of food. Here in Gilgal there wasn't enough food for everybody and this lack sets the stage for God's intervention in their lives. Under the Old Covenant famines were not a regular occurrence nor were they normal events in the history of Israel. 2 Kings 8:1 says, "For the Lord has called for a famine."

Why did He do that? The law of Moses said in Deut. 11:16,17 that the presence of a famine was a manifestation of God's judgment against the people for their unrepentant idolatry. There was a three-and-a-half-year famine during the time of Elijah (1 Kings 18:2) but it did not produce lasting repentance from the people. The Lord then decides to discipline them even further. 2 Kings 8:1 further tells us that the people of the land were in the midst of a seven-year famine, twice as long as the punishment that came against them when Elijah was alive. What we learn from this is that to revisit sins that we have vowed to never entertain invites greater discipline from our loving Father. He loves us too much to keep us in our sin. Heb. 12:7,8 (MSG) says, "This trouble you're in isn't punishment; it's training, the normal experience of children. Only irresponsible parents leave children to fend for themselves."

Deception comes in when people think since they've survived the consequences of their sin in the past, they'll just go ahead and commit the same sin again. They think they can get away with sin, forgetting the words of Gal. 6:7, "Do not be deceived, God is not mocked; for whatever a man sows, that he will also reap." The Amplified Bible says, "God will not allow Himself to be sneered at, scorned, disdained, or mocked by mere pretensions or professions, or by His precepts being set aside." There is always a price to pay for sin. Novelist Robert Louis Stevenson, author of the novel "Treasure Island," once said, "Sooner or later in life, we all sit down to a banquet of consequences." When it comes to sin, God will not treat you indifferent just because you're a Christian. The truth be told, the discipline may be more harsh because you should know better.

Here in 2 Kings 4 the people of God rebelled and increased in apostasy by abandoning their beliefs. They didn't learn the first time so God now sends them a famine twice as long. God is a loving Father so let's not forget the words of Prov. 3:12, "For the Lord disciplines the one He loves, as does a father the son in whom he delights." God is very calculating in how He deals with you as His child. He loves you too much to let you keep on sinning. Therefore, He changes things around you in order to change you. The good news is we have a God who supplies the needs of those who are faithful to Him even in the midst of a famine. Here in Gilgal there are a remnant of true believers. Vs. 38, "Now the sons of the prophets were sitting before him." These were prophets in training and sitting before Elisha is a posture of being humble and ready to receive instruction.

This was a very severe famine and the bodies of the people looked despicable in their skeletal conditions. So desperate were they for food that some boiled their children and ate them (2 Kings 6:29). In the marketplace people were buying the heads of donkeys which were unclean animals and dove droppings for food. The people not only ate these things but paid dearly for them (2 Kings 6:25). And in the midst of this national life-changing drought are a group of men called "the sons of the prophets" sitting in front of Elisha learning from him as much as they can. In other words, school is still in session. With humility and eagerness they have a deep desire to receive wisdom and insight and knowledge from the man of God before them. To his credit, Elisha was faithful and loving enough to provide it. As hunger ravished the land, here in Gilgal a spiritual feast was taking place at the same time.

The posture of these men remind us of a truth proclaimed by Jesus in Matt. 4:4, "Man shall not live by bread alone, but by every word that proceeds from the mouth of God." What Jesus is saying here as He quoted Deut. 8:3 is that you cannot know the fullness of life if all you do is pursue material provisions and the fleshly desires of this world. You can only unlock what Jesus calls the abundant life (John 10:10) by positioning yourself to receive constant nourishment from His Word for this is the real source of life. All of our blessings and physical needs come to us because of God's divine provision. When we are deprived of life's necessities we must depend on God to meet our daily needs. At the same time, we must do what the sons of the prophets did as they went through the same famine as everyone else, study and obey the Word and sit before the man of God.

Those who desire to live by bread alone will never tap into the true riches of God. They will never possess all that God wants to give them because they are not convinced of their need for Him. Without a deep commitment to God and His Word people will shrivel up on the inside. Temptation becomes stronger and the things of the world become more enticing and seductive to their flesh. These are the people who boil their children for food and eat the heads of donkeys and dove dung. They're not like the sons of the prophets who are energized by the words spoken to them by Elisha. These godly men were impacted by the famine but not overcome by it. Notice what Elisha said to his servant in vs. 38, "Put on the large pot, and boil stew for the sons of the prophets." This was not a gourmet meal they're having. Vs. 39, "So one went out into the field to gather herbs, and found a wild vine, and gathered from it a lap full of wild gourds."

Gourds were a squash-like plant renowned for their exceptional decorative appearance. They have a sweet taste when not fully grown but become bitter the longer they grow. This servant didn't know what these gourds were but picked them anyway. Vs. 39 says he "came and sliced them into the pot of stew, though they did not know what they were." The ingredients put into this pot of stew reveal this is not a royal banquet they're going to partake in. These faithful men of God were not completely exempt from the sufferings around them. Why is that? Because God will sometimes allow His people to taste some of the sufferings of the world for the purpose of sanctification, to help us become more like Christ (Heb. 10:14). The good news is He will never abandon us or forsake us in these conditions. He will always be near and close enough to provide for our needs and to move on our behalf.

Unknown to those preparing the stew, gourds are a non-edible vegetable not suitable for eating no matter how long you steam or boil it. They look like squash but are not eaten like squash. Unfortunately, gourds are harmful and will poison the food these men are about to eat. They had a passion for the things of God but their ignorance of real-life skills cannot be justified. The pursuit of spiritual knowledge should not cause you to overlook the pursuit of practical wisdom and the general knowledge of this world that pertain to daily living. Being spiritual does not mean God called you to be ignorant in your dealings with the affairs of life. A lack of knowledge in these areas can put yourself and others in grave danger. So serious were these men in their service to the Lord that they became disabled in other crucial areas of life. They were very sincere but, in this case, they were sincerely wrong.

We also learn here that you cannot make good judgments based on appearance only. These gourds looked good and without any investigation the servant picked them and put them in the stew. By doing this he put himself and others in great peril. Just because something looks good does not mean it is. The Bible says that even the devil comes as an angel of light (2 Cor. 11:14). Also, this servant should have at least been suspicious as to why the gourds were there in the first place. They were in a famine so why had they not been already picked? The answer, of course, is that others knew how toxic they were and left them alone. Because this servant let his guard down, he introduced himself and others to something that was harmful. Ignorance is very dangerous. It can even be deadly. Philosopher Karl Popper said, "True ignorance is not the absence of knowledge, but the refusal to acquire it."

"Then they served it to the men to eat. Now it happened, as they were eating the stew, that they cried out and said, 'O man of God, there is death in the pot!' And they could not eat it" (vs. 40). Something was not right and immediately they cried out to the man of God. They are to be commended for this because Elisha was God's representative and was symbolic of the Word of God. These sons of the prophets knew where to go for help, trusting that Elisha would have the solution to their dilemma. They were right and the man of God told them what to do. "So he said, 'Then bring some flour.' And he put it into the pot, and said, 'Serve it to the people, that they may eat.' And there was nothing harmful in the pot" (vs. 41). It took faith for the sons of the prophets to now eat this stew for flour does not have the capability to remove poison. Their faith was not in the flour but in the God Elisha represented.

What was the solution to this problem specifically and all problems generally? The Word of the Lord! The word from Elisha's mouth was just as powerful as the written Word of God. Elisha was very calm while all this was going on. His eyes were on God and he knows he serves a God of provision, a God who has the answer to every problem he faces. There is no hint of worry and no hint of fear. By faith he's walking with God and this is an opportunity for him to display his faith in the awesome, supernatural power of God. The truth be told, in one form or another, famines come to everyone. The good news is that famines are material for a miracle. No matter what your difficulty is, God can move on your behalf. Famines are an opportunity for you to lean into God and put your faith to work. It's an opportunity for God to reveal to you His faithfulness when you put your trust in Him.

When a famine comes your way, your confidence will tell a watching world that you've got a God who takes care of you. You display your faith by being peaceful and calm during your ordeal. Is. 26:3,4 says, "You will keep him in perfect peace, whose mind is stayed on You, because he trusts in You. Trust in the Lord forever, for in YAH, the Lord, is everlasting strength." Famines give you an opportunity to hear God's voice. Prov. 1:18 says, "Wisdom calls aloud in the street; She raises her voice in the open squares," in the intersections of life. God is saying, "I'm right here if you'll only trust Me to supply all your needs." We now come across a second story that emphasizes the fact that God provides in famine. 2 Kings 4:42 says, "Then a man came from Baal Shalisha, and brought the man of God bread of the firstfruits, twenty loaves of barley bread, and newly ripened grain in the knapsack."

The region of Shalisha is only mentioned in the Bible in 1 Sam. 9:4 which tells the story of Saul passing through this area in search of his father's lost donkeys. But here this region is called Baal Shalisha. This is heartbreaking because it tells of the decline of Israel's fidelity to the Lord as they renamed the region after a false god. It is quite possible that this area was a worship center to demonic deity. And it was from this region that a man came to help the few ministers of God who remained in Israel. Even in a famine this man is bringing the firstfruits to the man of God based on Deut. 18:4, "The firstfruits of your grain, of your wine and of your oil, and the first fleece of your sheep you shall give him." The law said the firstfruits were to go to the priests of the tribe of Levi but this man brought his offering to Elisha. Why? Because he could not find a priest who had not been compromised.

This man from Baal Shalisha is trying to obey what God asks of him to the best of his ability. He found in Elisha a faithful minister to whom he could give his offering to. This man is to be highly commended. He had every reason not to give to the work of the Lord. There was a famine in the land plus he could not find a priest worthy to receive the first-fruits. He didn't want to wait to honor God at another time, he wanted to honor God now. He then chose to express his devotion by seeking out Elisha, believing God would be pleased in this. This man puts to shame all those who make excuses for their disobedience. True worship is when you do all you can to honor God, even if it means to go out of your way to do so. God is worthy to be recognized and honored, and the man did just that. He gave his offering to Elisha whose Christlike character shines again when he says, "Give it to the people, that they may eat" (vs. 42).

He didn't focus on his own hunger but on the well-being of the sons of the prophets. This is what true leadership looks like, when you're devoted to the care of those under your authority. "But the servant said, 'How can I set this before a hundred men?' So he repeated, 'Give it to the people that they may eat, for thus says the Lord, "They shall eat and have some left over" (vs. 43). This command didn't make sense to the man from Baal Shalisha but these are the moments when God shines the brightest. He's the God of the impossible, the God of things that don't make sense. The man chose to obey Elisha even though he questioned the possibility of feeding a hundred men. We learn here that faith doesn't have to understand, it only has to obey. It was his obedience that brought forth an amazing miracle. Vs. 44 says, "So he set it before them; and they ate and had some left over, according to the word of the Lord."

| 11 |

"WHITE AS SNOW"

A sad truth in life is that most of God's people are missing out on God's miracles because they won't believe. They have the capacity to believe but choose not to. Why? Because they spend too much time blaming God for their troubles and questioning why things happen the way they do. They don't rise up in faith and do something about it. Consider what Jesus said in Luke 4:27, "And many lepers were in Israel in the time of Elisha the prophet, and none of them were cleansed except Namaan the Syrian." The Jewish lepers of Elisha's day, and there were many, were not cleansed because there was no faith in them. Jesus, however, points out that a Gentile from a distant country did. Take comfort knowing that God will do miracles in response to your faith. Jesus told us of an army commander who received his miracle and his story is found in 2 Kings 5:1-14.

The archives of miracles performed by Elisha is vast and long but the one miracle he is arguably best known for is the healing of Naaman, a story we can learn a lot from. Out of all the miraculous things Elisha had done, this particular miracle is the only thing mentioned in the New Testament when Jesus was rebuking His doubters. It, therefore, becomes imperative that we take a close look at the healing of Naaman for in this story is found the key to experiencing the miracle-working power of God. 2 Kings 5:1 says, "Now Naaman, commander of the army of the king of Syria, was a great and honorable man in the eyes of his master, because by him the Lord had given victory to Syria." Right away we learn that Naaman is an impressive individual. He is highly achieved and greatly respected. Vs. 1 continues, "He was also a mighty man of valor, but he was a leper."

Notice that this verse tells us right away what the source of Naaman's stellar resume was. It says the Lord working through him was the reason for Syria's victory. This takes on more meaning when you realize that Naaman was a Gentile and not a Jew. He is called a mighty man of valor, a title given to many of Israel's greatest kings, judges, and warriors. Naaman was an outsider and this tells us that the Lord is active and at work beyond the boundaries of Israel, proving that He is forever sovereign over everything. In other words, God is always on the move even beyond the community of faith, outside of those Jews who were in covenant with Him. To the Jews, this was unprecedented. How shocked they must have been to know that God had concern for the Gentiles. This forced the people of Israel to reconsider the extent of the goodness of God.

It is the duty of every person to acknowledge with a heart of worship that God is the one who gives people the energy, the intellect, and the time to fully carry out His will. Naaman was a great man and a mighty warrior but, unfortunately, he had leprosy, a severe skin disease that leads to a deterioration and disfigurement of the body. Leprosy was a horrible, dreaded disease. The first person in the Bible affected with leprosy was Miriam, the sister of Moses, a punishment she received for criticizing her brother (Num. 12:10). Miriam became "white as snow, as one dead, whose flesh is half consumed when he comes out of his mother's womb!" (vs. 10,12). Leprosy made her look like a rotting corpse. People with leprosy were in horrible pain and were a despicable sight to look at. They were cut off from their families and all social gatherings, living a life of total seclusion.

This story tells us that no matter how well off you are, you are not exempt from the effects of the fall of man. Jesus said in Matt. 5:45 that it rains on the just and unjust. It was a curse for any person to have leprosy. They were pushed away and set aside. They were mocked, ridiculed, and despised by others. They had no hope for a normal life. Still, Naaman socialized with others as if he did not have this disease. Perhaps it was his reputation and high standing with the king that allowed this to happen. The Bible also doesn't say how far along Naaman's leprosy was, if it was in the early or latter stages of its consumption. Either way, he had little hope at this moment. Unknown to him, that would soon change. Vs. 2,3 says, "And the Syrians had gone out on raids, and had brought back captive a young girl from the land of Israel. She waited on Naaman's wife. Then she said to her mistress, 'If only my master were with the prophet who is in Samaria! For he would heal him of his leprosy'" (vs. 2,3).

We don't know this girl's name but we do know she was torn away from her family during an act of war. It is quite possible that her parents were killed during this raid. She now finds herself serving the wife of the man responsible for the great loss she suffered. Instead of being bitter and resentful, she instead makes a bold statement of faith. This is a girl who has a forgiving, faith-filled spirit. She shows us here that walking in faith is not possible if your heart isn't right, that light and darkness don't mix. Because of the purity of her heart, this girl will play a crucial role in the redemption of many men. Because of her, the life of Naaman and countless others will never be the same.

The faith of this young girl is nothing short of amazing. She demonstrates a strong faith in God even though as a slave she is the least influential person in the entire nation. Her trust in God shaped her composure and strengthened her witness. Like this girl, let your faith in God determine how you interpret, engage, and experience all the affairs of life. This girl needs to be ranked alongside all the other faithful saints in scripture who had a righteous influence in pagan nations, people like Joseph, Esther, and Daniel. They were all exiles taken out of their homeland and still God used them mightily. Because they remained faithful to God, they were able to make a remarkable impact in secular places. One thing different about this girl is that she never got promoted to a higher position like the others. She remained in obscurity and this is what makes her story so beautiful.

This little servant girl didn't receive the recognition she deserved but still was an instrument in the hands of God to make a powerful impact on someone else's life. This should be a source of great encouragement to you if you think you're not important enough to be used by God in a powerful way. If God used her, He can use you. For that to happen, like this girl you must be free from all bitterness and animosity toward those who have done you wrong. You can't let hatred and unforgiveness fill your heart. She was a slave who was snatched out of innocence but still she has no resentment in her heart. Instead, she exemplifies a spiritual godliness by wanting her master to be healed. Think about that. This is the man responsible for the probable death of her parents and here she is wanting to help him. There is no better example of Christlikeness than that.

This girl is also to be commended for knowing who Elisha was and where he was located. This reveals her understanding and awareness of God, proving her parents raised her well. How did she know Elisha could heal Naaman of his leprosy? Because she knew the character of God and how He used Elisha in times past to remove obstacles in people's lives. She had strong faith in God and was confident in suggesting that Naaman go see Elisha. Vs. 4 says Naaman then went to his master and told him what this girl from Israel said. "And the king of Syria said, 'Go now, and I will send a letter to the king of Israel.' So he went, taking with him ten talents of silver, six thousand shekels of gold, and ten changes of clothing" (vs. 5). Why is Naaman bringing all these riches with him? He is going into enemy territory, a place he had raided and brought death and harm to, and now he's going there asking for help.

He's probably thinking these gifts will persuade the king of Israel to grant him an audience with Elisha and that he is willing to pay for his healing. Clearly, he doesn't grasp the accessibility of faith. You don't have to pay money to have an audience with God and to obtain favor from Him. All you need is faith. Paul said about God in Acts 17:27, "He is not far from each one of us." Naaman did not understand this and he's hoping these gifts will weaken any resistance on Israel's part. Another mistake is made as he hands the letter from his king to the king of Israel. The letter said, "Now be advised, when this letter comes to you, that I have sent Naaman my servant to you, that you may heal him of his leprosy" (vs. 6). What's wrong here? The king can't heal anybody and he knows it. He tore his clothes and said, "Am I God, to kill and make alive, that this man sends a man to me to heal him of his leprosy?" (vs. 7).

The king is clearly overwhelmed by this request from the king of Syria. He misinterprets what's being said and goes so far to say, "See how he seeks a quarrel with me'" (vs. 7). This king is aware of the miracle-working power of God. The context suggests this is King Jehoram, one of three kings whose armies were delivered from thirst in 2 Kings 3. Apparently this miracle did not make a lasting impression on him. Instead of displaying the confidence that Elisha can help the man, he instead panics and tears his clothes. It is amazing that a young slave girl has more faith than the king of Israel. This shows how lowly, unfortunate people often have a faith greater than those who are well off. Elisha heard what the king had done so he sent word to him, "Why have you torn your clothes? Let him come now to me, that he may know that there is a prophet in Israel" (vs. 8).

This was a gentle rebuke to the king. He should have known what to do but instead he panicked and tore his clothes. Notice the faith of Elisha when he called for Naaman to be brought to him. The king is filled with fear while Elisha is filled with faith and confidence in his God. The king has no hope because, when you walk in unbelief, hope is hard to come by. "Then Naaman went with his horses and chariots, and he stood at the door of the house of Elisha" (vs. 9). This was not a quiet visit in the dark but a loud, noisy encounter in broad daylight. For sure, this was a massive entourage. Naaman was the commander of a large army and he's now in enemy territory. He's not traveling alone. Hundreds of men and horses are with him. Naaman now stands at the door of Elisha's humble home and he's probably expecting a warm welcome with opened arms from the prophet of God. To his surprise, this didn't happen.

Instead, vs. 10 says, "And Elisha sent a messenger to him, saying, 'Go and wash in the Jordan seven times, and your flesh shall be restored to you, and you shall be clean.'" These instructions were simple and straight forward. Do what the prophet said, and the leprosy would go away. But for Naaman, this was very anticlimactic, and he got very angry. He had traveled a great distance, and the prophet didn't even come out to acknowledge him. He's probably thinking, "What's going on here? Doesn't he know who I am?" This is pride in full manifestation. Elisha wasn't being inconsiderate here. He just perceived that Naaman had a bigger problem than leprosy that needed to be dealt with. Naaman was a man of pride and Elisha is going to help him be healed in this area also. Before Naaman could be healed of leprosy, he would first have to humble himself.

Micah 6:8 says, "He has shown you, O man, what is good; And what does the Lord require of you but to do justly, to love mercy, and to walk humbly with your God?" This is why Elisha didn't come out and greet Naaman face-to-face. He wasn't impressed with his rank and all the soldiers with him. He challenged what Naaman expected to happen. He was sending a message to this mighty man of valor that he needs to approach God in humility, lowliness, and brokenness. Don't come expecting things to be done your way. When God's word is made known to you, you become humble before God by aligning yourself to it no matter how much it challenges your preconceived notions and desires. This is what humbleness looks like. This is what God requires of you even if it challenges your flesh. Naaman's flesh resisted Elisha's instructions with great anger.

He went away furious and said, "Indeed, I said to myself, 'He will surely come out to me, and stand and call on the name of the Lord his God, and wave his hand over the place, and heal the leprosy'" (vs. 11). In his anger Naaman is stating what he thought should happen and that's the problem. Prov. 14:12 says, "There is a way that seems right to a man but its end is the way of death." The reality of life is that the thinking of too many people is killing them. It separates them from the goodness of God because they're too proud and too stubborn to do what the Word says. Naaman next complained about where this healing was to take place. He asked, "'Are not the Abanah and the Pharpar, the rivers of Damascus, better than all the waters of Israel? Could I not wash in them and be clean?' So he turned away in a rage."

| 12 |

"OUT OF CONTROL"

The purpose of miracles is to bring about radical change, both externally and internally. Naaman's skin had just been cleansed of leprosy, and his heart was cleansed also. Because of this miracle, Naaman's faith will be converted to the true and living God. Never will his life be the same because of the remarkable transformation of his inner convictions. After being cleansed, Naaman went and stood before Elisha and said, "Indeed, I know that there is no God in all the earth but in Israel; so accept now a gift from your servant" (2 Kings 5:15). Out of his gratitude he wants to leave a gift with the spiritual and human instrument God used to bring about his miracle. Notice how in humility he even called himself Elisha's servant. Here is one of the most notable Gentile converts in all the Old Testament. A genuine conversion had taken place in his heart, and he returned to Elisha to tell him just that.

He made the same confession that a faithful Israelite would make, that there is no other God in all the earth. Unlike other pagans, he did not add this God to the other gods he worshipped. He aligned his heart with the exclusivity of the God of Israel, shunning his belief in other gods. This is a massive declaration for somebody with his background to make. Another noteworthy thing Naaman did is he returned to the prophet Elisha and demonstrated a willingness to respond sacrificially to the experience he had with the grace of God. He could have traveled right away back to Syria, but he didn't. Instead, he traveled many miles out of his way to come before the man of God to show him his deep gratitude. Naaman went above and beyond what most people would have done in order to properly respond to the miraculous encounter he had with the living God of Israel.

For good reason, Elisha rejected his offer. Vs. 16 says, "But he said, 'As the Lord lives, before whom I stand, I will receive nothing.' And he urged him to take it, but he refused." Why did Elisha reject Naaman's gift when he willingly accepted without reservation the services of the Shunammite woman? Clearly there was a reason for this happening. Naaman was a Gentile and Elisha discerned it was not the proper time to receive his gift (vs. 26). He didn't want to give Naaman the impression that this miracle was somehow earned or purchased. Then Naaman said, "If not, please let your servant be given two mule-loads of earth, for your servant will no longer offer burnt offering or sacrifice to other gods, but to the Lord" (vs. 17). Naaman wants to carry a piece of Israel back home with him as a physical reminder of his newfound faith and the exclusive devotion he pledges to the Lord above.

He believed that when he spread this dirt from Israel over a portion of Syrian ground that it would become holy ground and render it suitable for the worship of God. His open declaration that he will never again offer sacrifices to any other God reveals the genuine depth of his commitment to God and the sincerity of his conversion. Notice also that he says to Elisha three times that he is the prophet's servant. This is God at work. He'll first make you a saint and then He'll make you a servant. The effects of the gospel in this regard are repetitive throughout the New Testament. Titus 2:14 says those who have been redeemed will be "zealous for good works." When you're saved, you're going to want to serve God and His people with unmeasurable eagerness and joy. Your highest goal is to advance the kingdom of God on planet earth.

Naaman is now a new man. His conscience is changing and he's now becoming more sensitive to spiritual matters that he had never been concerned about before. As he made his way from the Jordan River to the man of God it weighed heavily on his mind how his new way of life would conflict with his responsibilities back in Syria. Naaman is deeply bothered because he's going back home to a place that worships false gods and he wants to express his concern openly with Elisha in hopes of gaining some type of assurance. He said, "When my master goes into the house of Rimmon to worship there, leaning on my arm, and I bow myself to the house of Rimmon, may the Lord please pardon your servant in this thing" (vs. 18). Apparently, the king of Syria was an elderly man and needed Naaman's assistance to help him bow down to worship the false god Rimmon. This would in turn cause Naaman to position himself in a similar fashion.

Naaman was concerned about this and he's asking for the Lord to pardon him in the performance of his duties. He's saying he's bowing on the outside but not on the inside. What we will learn from Elisha's response is that mature believers must not be too stiff and rigid or legalistic in the way they counsel and advise people in various predicaments. In other words, not everything in life is black and white. Yes, there are things in scripture that are clear and undisputable. There are, however, some things that are not as straight forward as we would like. These are the gray areas of life. They're neither black or white and godly wisdom must be used in giving counsel in these areas. If the wrong advice is given, great damage can be done. Be careful in how you apply God's Word in situations that don't have a Bible verse to tell you what should be done. Ask God to help you be as close as possible to His will and purpose.

Naaman anticipates in advance that he would have to compromise, at least in appearance, his allegiance to the Lord when he resumes his role as servant to the king of Syria. One is reminded of Obadiah in 1 Kings 18 who feared God but managed to retain the confidence of King Ahab as one of his chief officials. He remained faithful to God in a Baal-loving court. Elisha did not approve or disapprove of the conviction which Naaman expressed. He did believe the good seed already sown in Naaman's heart would grow and bear good fruit in due season. Perhaps in time Naaman would be able to introduce his king to the God of Israel. So, what did Elisha say to Naaman? "Go in peace" (vs. 19). This is all he said. Nothing more, nothing less. It is a wonderful thing that Elisha replied as gently as he did. This was more than a polite farewell. He is saying that the peace of God will go with him as he returned home.

Elisha is saying to let peace be your guide in matters such as this. Let peace give you divine direction for it is the inner confirmation that God approves of the decision you have made. Col. 3:15 (AMP), "And let the peace and soul harmony which comes from Christ rule and act as umpire continually in your hearts, deciding and settling with finality all questions that arise in your minds." God gives His people peace in order to guide them in making right decisions that line up with His will. A lack of peace should get your attention and will help you avoid missing the mark. Pray and seek God's guidance and then take notice how you feel when you've made a certain decision. If you sense peace, it's a sign you're in alignment with God's will. But if there's unrest and confusion, it might be time to pause and seek further guidance. Ps. 37:5 says, "Let the Lord be your guide into the future. Trust in Him and He will help you."

With his heart and body now cleansed, Naaman begins his long journey back to Syria. Hopefully his recent experience will help him abstain from all appearances of evil. Unfortunately, Elisha's servant Gehazi did not do this. While Naaman experienced an inner cleansing, the heart of Gehazi was filled with inner decay. A sobering story now takes place. Gehazi had been Elisha's servant for a long time and had seen many miracles. Proximity to the things of God is a good thing. Being close to what God is doing should bring growth and maturity to your life. As Naaman found out, spiritual growth happens when God works in you and not just around you. Your heart gets softened and you're open and receptive to God's transforming power. But when greed and stubbornness set in, your heart will get hardened to the things of God and this can be a very deadly thing. You'll become cold and callous, insensitive to all spiritual matters.

Having a heart that is stone cold will cause you to be prideful as you rationalize the comings and goings of everyday life. The only thing you'll be concerned about is yourself and nobody else. It bothered Gehazi that Elisha did not accept the offered gift from Naaman for the cleansing miracle he experienced. It weighed heavily on his mind until an evil plot formed in his thinking. Naaman had departed and was about five miles away when Gehazi said to himself, "As the Lord lives, I will run after him and take something from him" (Vs. 20). So he pursued Naaman. This was clearly in defiance of the wishes of Elisha, the man of God. He even had the audacity to invoke the name of God in this matter as if he had the Lord's approval. On top of all that, he was even criticizing the decision-making abilities of Elisha. He didn't think the prophet knew what he was doing and decided to take matters into his own hands.

The moment Naaman pulls away in his chariot, Gehazi lets the devil go to work in his mind. Instead of thinking how awesome God is, he is lured and enticed by his own desires. James 1:14 (TPT), "It is each person's own desires and thoughts that drag them into evil and lure them away into darkness." MSG, "We have no one to blame but the leering, seducing flare-up of our own heart." Gehazi did not view Naaman as a fellow worshipper of God but as somebody he could get something from. In his mind was a picture of great riches being heaped upon him. It never enters the mind of a true servant of God what people can give them. Their only concern is the spiritual change and development of the people they're trying to help. A true servant of God will trust God to meet their needs and take care of them as they focus on meeting the needs of others. They know God is their source of supply, not people.

Never be like Gehazi who looked at ministry as a platform for financial gain. This is a very dangerous thing to do for it will certainly bring about your downfall. The truth be told, Gehazi should have known better. As Elisha's personal assistant, he saw in the man of God that it was possible to be consistently holy before God. In spite of all the righteous things he had seen and heard, he still caved in to covetousness. We learn from this that special spiritual advantages do not guarantee personal change. Yes, living in the midst of the miraculous can promote growth and change but, ultimately, the choice to be influenced depends solely on the heart of each individual. Gehazi had seen and heard it all, yet his heart was filled with wickedness. One is reminded of Judas Iscariot who followed Jesus for three years and still sold Him out for thirty pieces of silver.

Gehazi's craving for financial gain caused him to devalue the man of God. He said in vs. 20, "My master should not have let the Syrian get away without accepting any of his gifts." He was saying Elisha was a fool for not accepting payment for Naaman's miracle. He thought he had more discernment in this matter than the anointed prophet of God. What does the Bible say about this? "Woe to those who call evil good and good evil, who turn darkness to light and light to darkness, who replace bitter with sweet and sweet with bitter" (Is. 5:20). So deceived was Gehazi that he falsely believed it was God's will for him to pursue financial gain for this miracle. This was a clear indication that he did not fear God or have reverence for Him. Gehazi's addiction to materialism was so great that he said he would exert all his energy to run after and catch up to Naaman who was a few short miles away at this time.

Here is an example of a man showing greater excitement and enthusiasm for personal gain than for spiritual maturity and influence. If only he showed the same dedication for the things of God. Money was Gehazi's god and not the true God of Israel. Vs. 21, "So Gehazi pursued Naaman. When Naaman saw him running after him, he got down from the chariot to meet him, and said, 'Is all well?'" Naaman was the commander of the Syrian army yet he gets down off his chariot to meet Gehazi on his level. This humility shows that his transformation was real and not superficial. Gehazi is now looking at Naaman face to face and what's the first thing he does? He lies to him about himself, Elisha, and the sons of the prophets. He is lying to a brand new believer. He answered and said, "All is well" (vs. 22). This is the lie about himself. He is self-deceived because he is far from being well. He is not being honest about his spiritual condition.

Gehazi continued, "My master has sent me to say, 'There have just come to me two young men of the sons of the prophets. Please give them a talent of silver and two changes of clothes'" (vs. 22). Did Elisha send Gehazi to Naaman? No. Gehazi is lying and misrepresenting the man of God. Did two men come from the hills of Ephraim? No, he's also lying about the sons of the prophets. This tells us that when a man is consumed with greed, he rarely, if ever, becomes an honest person in the process. Instead, he will lie and manipulate people for the purpose of personal gain. The truth is, Gehazi was a skilled deceiver. He used the guise and assumed appearance of a charitable work to request a donation from Naaman. He used trickery for selfish purposes. "So Naaman said, 'Please take two talents'" (vs. 23). Naaman is a changed man, and he offers to give Gehazi twice the amount he asked for. He even urged him to take the money.

"And he urged him, and bound two talents of silver in two bags, with two changes of garments, and handed them to two of his servants; and they carried them on ahead of him" (vs. 23). This was a sizable donation because it took two servants to carry all the silver that was given. Gehazi now knows he has to escape the supervision of Elisha to make his evil scheme work. "When he came to the hill, he took them from their hand and stored them away in the house; then he let the men go, and they departed" (vs. 24). Notice he didn't let these servants go near Elisha. What happened next? "Now he went in and stood before his master. And Elisha said to him, 'Where did you go, Gehazi?' And he said, 'Your servant did not go anywhere'" (vs. 25). He lied to Naaman to get this donation and now he lies to Elisha. This is how cover-ups spin out of control. One lie demands another until the truth explodes with disastrous ramifications.

One can understand Gehazi having the nerve to lie to Naaman but not to Elisha the prophet of God. As he will soon find out, the longer sin is hidden, the more severe its exposure. Elisha said to him, "Did not my heart go with you when the man turned back from his chariot to meet you?" (vs. 26). God revealed to Elisha every move Gehazi made. People who don't fear God think they can get away with anything and keep secrets in their life not knowing Num. 32:23, "You have sinned against the Lord, and be sure your sin will find you out." One of the greatest fuels to sin is secrecy but hidden sin is always exposed. What begins in the heart, things such as greed, envy, and deception, will eventually be revealed. Elisha asked, "Is it time to receive money and to receive clothing, olive groves and vineyards, sheep and oxen, male and female servants?" (vs. 26). He is telling Gehazi he knows what his secret ambitions are.

Gehazi only took money and clothing but ultimately he wanted land, flocks of animals, servants, comfort, and influence. He coveted all these things and used the ministry as a means to get them. Little did he know that secret sins will always rob you of your calling and bring with it severe judgment. Standing before the man of God, Gehazi now learns what his fate will be. Elisha said to him, "Therefore the leprosy of Naaman shall cling to you and your descendants forever." And he went out from his presence leprous, as white as snow (vs. 27). Gehazi wanted Naaman's money, now he gets Naaman's leprosy. His secret sin of greed and deceit led to a devastating public judgment, one that will cling to his descendants for generations to come. Gehazi lost any potential to be used by God in a most significant way, and his sin brought havoc to his home. When you consider the pain that sin brings, it will be less attractive than walking in righteousness.

| 13 |

"LITTLE PROBLEMS"

If there is one thing a lot of people don't know about God, it's that He cares about the little things in our life, things so small that we hesitate to approach Him about them. We have no problem asking for big help with our big problems, not realizing that He is anxious and more than willing to give us big help for our little problems. 2 Kings 6:1-7 tells of a miracle that most commentators say very little about because they think it is not as significant as all the other miracles recorded in the Bible. They think the problem this miracle solved was too small to give it the time and attention it so rightfully deserves. But know this, this story was put here to teach us a very valuable lesson. We shall see that this miracle and the story behind it is extremely important because it shows us that God's power meets us at the point of our need, no matter how small it may be.

This story takes place during a time of political unrest in the land of Israel. The people's lives were unstable because of rampant idolatry and a growing abandonment of spiritual beliefs. In the midst of this moral darkness was a remnant of faithful believers who did not succumb to a culture that was rapidly growing indifferent to the things of God. Prophetic schools were growing and young men were being trained under the guidance of Elisha. So fast was this growth that more space to live and study was needed. "And the sons of the prophets said to Elisha, 'See now, the place where we dwell with you is too small for us'" (vs. 1). This was a problem they were willing to solve with their own hands. They said, "'Please, let us go to the Jordan, and let every man take a beam from there, and let us make there a place where we may dwell.' And he answered, 'Go'" (vs. 2).

This building project initiated by these young men was a testament to their commitment to God and the prophet Elisha. To their credit they were not deterred by the downfall of Gehazi. These students were laser-focused and committed more than ever. They didn't slow down and turn back on their calling. No, they kept their eyes on the Lord and marched on. These men should be an inspiration to all of us. Unfortunately, sins and failures committed by people who claim to serve God, even spiritual leaders, is not a rare occurrence. At some point in your life, you will be let down by someone who bears the name of Christ, and this may include, God forbid, a major worldwide leader of spiritual influence. It is quite possible that Gehazi was being trained to take the place of Elisha just like Elisha was trained under Elijah. This means his spiritual collapse was no small matter.

If and when something like this happens, determine to be like the sons of the prophets who committed themselves to serving God wholeheartedly even when others fell away. Another thing to consider is that it may have been Gehazi's downfall that led to the renewed energy and spiritual vigor and robustness displayed by the sons of the prophets. Sometimes a spiritual cleansing in the house of God has to take place before growth and revival can happen. Light and darkness don't mix and with Gehazi gone the true light can shine forth. One is reminded of when "Jesus went into the temple of God and drove out all who bought and sold in the temple and overturned the tables of the moneychangers and the seats of those who sold doves" (Matt. 21:12). What was He doing? He was cleaning house. The people were using the temple for something it was not designed for. They turned God's house of prayer into a den of thieves, and a cleansing had to take place.

Notice what happened next. "Then the blind and lame came to Him in the temple, and He healed them" (vs. 14). After Jesus cleaned house, the power of God was manifested. It is not uncommon in God's purging work for Him to remove those who hinder personal and collective growth, those who bring no spiritual benefit to the body of Christ. Jesus said of the Father in John 15:2, "Every branch in Me that does not produce fruit He removes; and every branch that bears fruit He prunes, that it may bear more fruit." In His sovereignty, one of the things God assures those who are truly abiding in Him is that He will cut away anyone or anything that prevents them from reaching their full potential. Gehazi got pruned from the house of God and suddenly the number of the sons of the prophets grew exceedingly, so much so that they needed a new building to be trained in.

It is at this time that they asked Elisha for permission to build a new dwelling place. It is one thing to recognize a need, another thing to volunteer to be an answer to that need. Their suggestion was to go to the Jordan River and build a bigger place there. When you go to the church leaders with a problem, try to bring a prayed-up solution with you. Notice also that everybody got involved in this project. They said, "Let us go to the Jordan and each of us get there a log." The only way to see significant growth is to have an "each of us" mentality. A handful of people doing the work will not get you very far. Everybody needs to be involved and do their part. Matt. 9:37 says, "The harvest truly is plentiful, but the laborers are few." Great needs bring with it great opportunities. Consistently look for ways to offer your time, talents, and resources to those in the local church and the worldwide kingdom of God.

Many hands make for light work and the "each of us" mentality causes people to lift up willing hearts and ready hands, saying, "Let us rise up and build" (Neh. 2:18). This was the attitude of the sons of the prophets. Everybody got involved because they knew that "two are better than one, because they have a good reward for their labor" (Eccl. 4:9). Eph. 4:16, "He makes the whole body fit together perfectly. As each and every part does its job, He makes the body grow so that it is healthy and full of love." Gehazi showed us that selfishness will suck the life out of any ministry. These men showed us that when we unselfishly work together, the work of the Lord gets done. These students had a plan and were ready to work hard and diligently on the task at hand. Their actions show the importance of dedication and effort in achieving success.

As they prepared to go to the Jordan River, one of them said to Elisha, "Please consent to go with your servants." And he answered, "I will go." So he went with them (vs. 3,4). They wanted the man of God involved in this work. They recognized that Elisha has a special connection with God and knew they could benefit from his ongoing counsel and guidance. Great benefits come when you associate with faith-filled people. It is a known fact that many of the things that happen to you is based on the company you keep. Prov. 12:26, "The righteous choose their friends carefully." This is good advice because you will become like the people you are connected to. Choose your friends, choose your future. The sons of the prophets had the wisdom to want Elisha in their presence as much as possible. No matter the task, always strive to have God's people alongside you.

Always invite God into your daily routines, whether it be preparing a Bible lesson or fixing a leaking pipe. Even mundane tasks can carry eternal significance when God is involved. Determine to never begin any project without praying and asking God to be a part of it. Ps. 127:1 says, "Unless the Lord builds the house, they labor in vain who build it." These men had the land, the wood, and the tools to build this new dwelling place but they would not begin without the Lord's blessing, represented by Elisha the prophet. "And when they came to the Jordan, they cut down trees" (vs. 4). The building project begins when suddenly, in the midst of their industrious endeavor, an unexpected crisis unfolds. "But as one was cutting down a tree, the iron ax head fell into the water; and he cried out and said, 'Alas, master! For it was borrowed'" (vs. 5).

The outcry of this man after the ax head sank into the depths of the Jordan River echoes not only the loss of a tool but also the weight of responsibility for this tool was borrowed. The land of Israel was in a season of need because of a famine that was taking place. The sons of the prophets barely had enough food to eat let alone the tools to build with. They were therefore forced to borrow some of the tools they needed to complete the task at hand. This shows us that God's servants are not always exempt from life's challenges. Matt. 5:45 says it rains on the just and on the unjust. The good news is that even in times of peril, God is still on the throne and no problem is too big or too small for Him to solve. It brings comfort to know that God cares about all our problems no matter what size they are. With God, there is no such thing as big problems. With Him, every problem is small.

In our way of thinking, a lost ax head is not as important as an incurable disease such as the leprosy suffered by Naaman. But it was important to this man and thus it was important to God. For sure, He cares about the things you care about. That's the God we love and serve. Ps. 136:1 says, "Oh give thanks to the Lord, for He is good! For His mercy endures forever." The word "mercy" Is often translated "loving devotion" and emphasizes the unending nature of God's divine kindness. The Hebrew word "chesed" refers to His steadfast love and covenant loyalty. In biblical theology, this word points to God's promise and unwavering commitment to sustain and protect His people. It speaks of intentional, faithful action. The Bible proclaims that God's goodness does not fail or falter even when our dire circumstances are extremely serious or urgent. His mercy is always there and has no limit.

Never think your need is too small to bring to God. He cares about your lost earring or your lost car keys. He cares if your washing machine is broken or if your lawn mower won't start. Jesus said, "Look at the birds of the air, for they neither sow nor reap nor gather into barns; yet your heavenly Father feeds them. Are you not of more value than they?" (Matt. 6:26). The bottom line is if it matters to you, it matters to God. Ps. 37:23 (NLT) says, "The Lord directs the steps of the godly. He delights in every detail of their lives." God wants you to be happy at all times. Ps. 32:11 says, "Be glad in the Lord, and rejoice, O righteous." If finding your lost ring will make you happy, He'll help you find it. The problem most people have with God is they don't understand how much He loves them, that He cares about the smallest details of their life, that He gives big help for little problems.

With much enthusiasm the sons of the prophets were hard at work chopping down trees. One of them, in his excitement, swung his ax back when suddenly the ax head flew off the handle. A moment later the man's heart sank as he watched it sink in the depths of the Jordan River. He cried out to Elisha, admitting the ax was borrowed. Literally it was "begged for." Notice the timing of this setback. This unfortunate incident happened when all the sons of the prophets were doing the right things. They were walking in faith and practicing humility. Each of them followed God and Elisha faithfully and instead of being lazy they rolled up their sleeves and went to work on this building project after getting permission to do so. After all that, something bad still happened. This tells us that we can never let our guard down where the devil is concerned. For sure, he never sleeps and he never slumbers.

This is why 1 Peter 5:8 says, "Be well balanced and always alert because your adversary the devil walks about like a roaring lion, seeking whom he may devour." AMP, "Be well balanced, temperate, sober of mind, be vigilant and cautious at all times; for that enemy of yours, the devil, roams around like a lion roaring in fierce hunger." The devil is not a joke or a cartoon, and he is not to be ignored. It is your responsibility to always be on the alert with a readiness to confront him at any given moment. Alertness is required because the devil rarely shows himself for who he really is. He comes as an angel of light and will strike unexpectedly when all appears to be going well. Be like the sons of the prophets who wanted God and His representative in the midst of what they were doing. With Elisha at their side, they knew where to turn when this crisis occurred.

Ex. 22:14 says if you lose something that is borrowed full restitution must be made. Clearly the man did not have the means to do this since the ax was borrowed in the first place. He was bothered by this and in his desperation, he cried out leaving himself open for any rebuke that may come his way. Perhaps he would be told to go into the water and find it himself. Thankfully, God is a God of mercy and this man's vulnerability opened the door for divine intervention. Cry out to God during your time of need for He responds to hearts that are humble and dependent on Him. 1 Peter 5:7 (AMP), "Casting all your cares, all your anxieties, all your worries, and all your concerns once and for all on Him, for He cares about you with deepest affection and watches over you very carefully." No, Elisha did not rebuke this man but simply asked, "Where did it fall?" (vs. 6). And the man showed him the place. Notice how Elisha's response to this crisis is marked by calm assurance.

He did not panic, nor did he get angry. Instead, he asked the man to show him the exact spot where the ax head fell knowing that restoration often begins where the loss occurred. God will ask you to revisit your point of loss in order to initiate recovery, whether it be something wrong you said, a bad decision you made, or a moment when you compromised your spiritual morals. Be willing to go back to where you missed the mark and admit your responsibility for what happened. Then you can ask God for help knowing He restores what you surrender, not what you cover up. God specializes in restoring what we thought was gone forever. Don't believe the lie that it's too late. Show Him the place you lost it and then cry out to Him in deep humility. Restoration starts at the point of failure. Trust Him to move beyond logic and into the miraculous, knowing His power is not limited to only big, grand, and dramatic problems.

Elisha then did something strange. Vs. 6 says he cut off a stick and threw it in the water where the ax head fell. In Hebrew it says he "shaped and sized" this branch. What is he doing here? Is it possible he's shaping this stick into a new ax handle to replace the old one? Are his actions telling us that to prepare for a miracle is part of receiving a miracle? James 2:26 says faith without works is dead. This is why married couples who are believing for a baby are encouraged to prepare a nursery for the child even before conception takes place. That is faith in action. This is what moves the hand of God. It took faith for Elisha to make this new ax handle. What happened next? "And he made the iron float" (vs. 6). This borrowed ax head defied the laws of nature and floated to the surface. There's even a strong possibility that Elisha's carved ax handle was attached to it.

Iron doesn't float but it did that day. This shows that God is not limited or bound by natural limitations when responding to faith and need. With Him, all things are possible. Faith is not limited when it's anchored in what's possible with God. This miracle is a powerful illustration of divine care even in what might seem like a trivial concern. God is a good God and He is willing to engage with His people in their daily challenges, offering restoration and assistance even in the seemingly mundane aspects of life. God created the laws of nature, and He can override them whenever He chooses. Elisha said to the man, "'Pick it up for yourself" (vs. 7). So he reached out his hand and took it. God not only performs miracles but also calls us to respond. The ax head floated but the man still had to reach out and take it. Miracles are God's work, obedience is ours.

| 14 |

"DIVINE REVELATION"

It is no secret to the body of Christ that they have a sworn, mortal enemy who continually roams around like a hungry roaring lion seeking whom he may devour (1 Peter 5:8). This is not a video game or a fairy tale but a very real war against a cunning, deceptive foe. Many are his schemes and cunning strategies to tempt, confuse, and ensnare individuals. These tactics are often aimed at leading believers astray from the path of righteousness and can include manipulation through temptation, threat, or intimidation. The devil in his wayward thinking has come up with evil plans, purposes, intentions, enterprises, and sly cunning ways to injure, take down, and destroy the souls of God-fearing people. John 8:44 says, "He is a liar and the father of lies." A fisherman uses bait to lure the fish onto the hook. Likewise, Satan uses appealing bait to disguise the hook of destruction.

Notice the bait the serpent used against Eve. He told her, "You shall not surely die. For God knows that in the day you eat of it your eyes will be opened, and you shall be like God" (Gen.

3:4,5). Thankfully, 2 Kings 6:8-12 shows us that the enemy has schemes, not surprises. We serve a God who makes known to us the plans of the enemy, that "we are not unaware of his devices" (2 Cor. 2:11). Vs. 8 tells us that "the king of Syria was making war against Israel, and he took counsel with his servants, saying, 'My camp will be in such and such a place.'" This was the same king who gave Naaman permission to go see Elisha as he sought deliverance from his leprosy. Surely Naaman brought back a good report and here the king is plotting against Israel. This king is filled with profound ingratitude for the miracle experienced by his military commander and has no regard for the people of Israel and, more importantly, the God of Israel.

The healing of Naaman left no lasting impression on the king of Syria. His country had continually plotted attacks against Israel in the past and here they are doing it once again. But this time things will be different. This time God will reveal to Elisha through divine revelation what the plans of the enemy were even though the king thought his strategies were secure. Awareness is protection. Vs. 9 says, "And the man of God sent to the king of Israel, saying, 'Beware that you do not pass this place, for the Syrians are coming down there.'" Awareness is strengthened when we live close to God. To be alert means to live with discernment through the Spirit. Security guards stay awake at night because vigilance is their defense. Awareness is vital to living a victorious life because spiritual sleepiness allows the enemy to gain ground. Matt. 41 says, "Watch and pray so that you will not fall into temptation."

The king of Syria devised plans to attack Israel but God revealed every detail to Elisha. It is futile to try to outwit God. No scheme or whisper in darkness escapes His eye. For sure, God sees what the enemy plots in secret. Job 34:21 says, "His eyes are on the ways of mortals; He sees their every step." Rest in the fact that God sees what we cannot. Revealing this evil scheme to Elisha is a testimony to the mercy of God considering the backslidden condition of Israel at this time and their idol-worshipping king, Jehoram, the son of Ahab. God did not completely abandon His people. He used Elisha to give them warnings and guidance and through that a steadfast invitation to be reconciled back to Him. "Then the king of Israel sent someone to the place of which the man of God had told him. Thus he warned him, and he was watchful there, not just once or twice" (vs. 10).

To his credit, Jehoram did the right thing at this point in time. Elisha's warnings were numerous, and the king's trust and obedience were consistent. He obeyed Elisha many times, not just once or twice. If he didn't obey, he would put himself and the people of Israel in extreme danger. If you want God's favor and protection in your life, then consider a single act of obedience as a deadly threat. Take holiness and all its rewards very seriously. Don't think you can nibble on sin and escape its deadly consequences. You cannot run away from the fact that there is always a price to pay for sin. It is foolish to trust in one's own wisdom and not on the Word of the Lord. On the day you got saved, you were called to a continual standard of dependency and reliance on God's Word. Prov. 3:5,6 says, "Trust in the Lord with all your heart and lean not on your own understanding; In all your ways acknowledge Him, and He shall direct your paths."

Trust and obey God's Word at all times. It's on the path of steadfast and faithful obedience that you'll find all the heavenly treasures of the continual favor and blessings of God. Because Elisha warned the king of Israel, the plans of their enemy continually failed. The king of Syria grew frustrated because he could not overpower the protection of God. This reveals that no weapon formed against God's people will ultimately prosper (Is. 54:17). The Lord not only informs us of the enemy's schemes, but He also secures our safety. Ps. 121:7 says, "The Lord will keep you from all harm; He will watch over your life." Don't live in fear of the enemy's plans. Instead, live in confidence of God's covering and protection. The king of Syria assumed human intelligence could outmaneuver God's people but every plan of his failed. This tells us that our victory is not based on human effort but on divine authority.

The enemy may plot in darkness, but God shines His holy light and exposes every scheme. The Hebrew word for "reveal" is "galah" and it means 'to uncover or disclose something hidden.' God takes an active role in making secrets known. Pray for Him to reveal to you hidden traps and attacks in your life. Thank Him for being your shield, your protector, your guide. Vs. 11, "Therefore the heart of the king of Syria was greatly troubled by this thing, and he called his servants and said to them, 'Will you not show me which of you is for the king of Israel?'" The king of Syria thought he had a traitor in his camp, but it wasn't a spy who betrayed him. It was the

Spirit of the Lord working through the prophet Elisha. "And one of his servants said, 'None, my lord, O king; but Elisha, the prophet who is in Israel, tells the king of Israel the words that you speak in your bedroom'" (vs. 12).

God gave Elisha supernatural foresight, and it devastated the work of the enemy. The king tried to hide his plans, but the Lord uncovered them proving that nothing is hidden from the eyes of God. When you walk closely with the Lord, He will give you revelation, discernment, guidance, and warning ahead of time. God whispers to His people, revealing things that no human could naturally know. Every trap laid against God's people is seen from heaven. The enemy may plot in secret, but God is always one step ahead of him. Trust that the Lord is watching out for you at all times. When the enemy schemes against you, remember that God already knows the plan and had made provision for your victory. Do not fear but believe that God is still protecting His people today. Man's secrets cannot bind God's purposes. The plots of darkness are powerless against the light of divine revelation. Stay close to God and He will protect you from what is planned against you.

The bottom line is God sees everything. Heb. 4:13, "Nothing in all creation is hidden from God. Everything is naked and exposed before His eyes, and He is the one to whom we are accountable." TPT, "There is not one person who can hide their thoughts from God, for nothing that we do remains a secret, and nothing created is concealed, but everything is exposed and defenseless before His eyes." A sad truth in life is that foolish people do foolish things. The king of Syria should have been humbled by what his servant said to him, that it is revealed what he says in his bedroom. But no, he was not humbled but instead foolishly devises another evil plot. "And he said, 'Go and see where he is, that I may send and seize him.' It was told him, 'Behold, he is in Dothan'" (vs. 13). The king is very frustrated and vs. 14 says what he did next, "Therefore he sent horses and chariots and a great army there, and they came by night and surrounded the city."

Notice that he didn't send a few soldiers but a whole force of military warriors. Think about that. One man full of God's power was considered a greater threat than an entire army. "When the servant of the man of God rose early in the morning and went out, behold, an army of horses and chariots was all around the city. And the servant said, 'Alas, my master! What shall we do?'" (vs. 15). Elisha's servant saw the size of the Syrian army and froze in fear. Instead of seeing the size of God, he saw the size of the problem. Fear blinds us to God's power and paralyzes our faith. This servant was afraid but not Elisha. He wasn't shaken and spoke words of reassurance. "So he answered, 'Do not fear, for those who are with us are more than those who are with them'" (vs. 16). Both Elisha and this servant who replaced Gehazi were facing the same threat. The difference between them was their perspective. The servant focused on what was seen, Elisha focused on what was unseen.

As we live horizontal lives it is of vital importance that we have vertical vision, that we see things from heaven's perspective. In God's kingdom, reality is not defined by what is seen. 2 Cor. 4:18 says, "We don't look for things that are seen, but for things that are not seen. Things that can be seen are only temporary. But the things that can't be seen last forever." The Bible makes it clear again and again that there is an unseen world that interacts with our natural world. The problem is people ignore vertical vision to their own detriment. Col. 3:2 says, "Set your mind on things above, not on the things that are on the earth." That's vertical vision. Heb. 12:2 says to fix your eyes on Jesus, the author and finisher of our faith. Elisha saw something his servant didn't see. He knew that the armies of heaven outnumbered the armies of Syria because he lived with the awareness that he was always in the presence of God.

His heart was tranquil and stabilized because of a promise found in Is. 26:3, "You will keep him in perfect peace whose mind is stayed on You, because he trusts in You." Elisha was not afraid. His heart was in perfect peace because his mind was always on the Lord. Unbroken peace from God is granted to those who have unbroken meditation on God. He lived in a reality that all believers should strive for. As people slowly but surely grow in their faith, they'll one day say with confidence, "If God be for us, who can be against us?" (Rom. 8:31). God's help is always there but fear keeps people blind. What they need is for God to open their eyes. "And Elisha prayed and said, 'Lord, I pray, open his eyes that he may see' Then the Lord opened the eyes of the young man, and he saw. And behold, the mountain was full of horses and chariots of fire all around Elisha" (vs. 17).

Many of God's people live in fear not knowing how close God's protection really is. Ps. 34:7 says, "The angel of the Lord encamps all around those who fear Him and delivers them." This verse is a promise of divine protection. It does not say trouble won't come because it will. What it does say is that when it does come God has already stationed His army around His people. The word "encamp" means 'to settle down; to pitch a tent; to remain.' This is not a passing visit but a permanent posting of God's angelic army. They surround you at all times. This is military language. God has assigned His angelic warriors to give you heavenly protection and to stand guard over your life. You are never alone, never unprotected, never abandoned. Notice that God's angelic protection is not a blanket promise to everyone but specifically to those who fear Him, to those who reverence and honor Him and live in obedience to Him.

David lifts the veil and reminds us that those who fear God are never alone. For sure, the safest place to be in this world is under the fear of the Lord, walking faithfully in His will. You may feel alone in your struggle, but if God were to open your spiritual eyes, you would see that you are never alone and never outnumbered. God's protection is closer than you realize. This heavenly army just didn't suddenly appear for it was already present. The servant just needed vertical vision, and Elisha loved him enough to ask God to give it to him. You can sense the earnestness of Elisha as he prayed with sincerity and longing. He shows us that there are certain levels of transformation that can only be achieved when we pray for people. Like Elisha here and Paul in the New Testament, you need to love your brothers and sisters in the Lord enough that you're willing to bring their needs and weaknesses before the throne of God.

Notice that when this servant's spiritual eyes were opened that he saw an angelic army "all around Elisha." These angels orbited around the man of God and extended outward to the hills. They weren't far off in the distance but right next to him as he stood by the side of Elisha. These were the same type of horses and chariots of fire that escorted Elijah to heaven. Just like they protected Elijah from death as he was being transported to heaven, these angelic beings also protected Elisha from death at the hands of the Syrian army. This story took place in Dothan; a city mentioned only one other time in the Old Testament. In Genesis 37 Jacob sent Joseph on a journey to see if all was well with his brothers "So he sent him out of the Valley of Hebron, and he went to Shechem. Now a certain man found him, and there he was, wandering in the field. And he asked him, 'What are you seeking?'" (vs. 14,15).

"So he said, 'I am seeking my brothers. Please tell me where they are feeding their flocks.' And the man said, 'They have departed from here, for I heard them say, "Let us go to Dothan"' So Joseph went up after his brothers and found them in Dothan. Now when they saw him afar off, even before he came near them, they conspired against him to kill him" (vs. 16-18). It was in Dothan where Joseph's brothers threw him into a pit and left him there like a wild animal. It was here that Joseph tasted the venomous envy and jealousy of his siblings. Dothan was the place where Joseph was abandoned by his family and the place where Elisha was ambushed by the enemy. The same protection that wrapped around Elisha also surrounded Joseph hundreds of years before. What happened twice in Dothan shows us that God is with us at all times, in all places, in every experience whether you are betrayed by loved ones or attacked by enemies.

Just as the Lord was with Joseph and Elisha, He is always there with you. Ps. 125:2 says, "As the mountains surround Jerusalem, so the Lord surrounds His people from this time forth and forevermore." If there's one thing people crave, it's security. They want to feel safe in their homes, their relationships, their finances, and in their future. Yet it is no secret that life can be extremely fragile. We live in a world filled with dangers, enemies of our faith, and unseen spiritual forces. The psalmist understood this but reminds us unequivocally that God's people are never alone. Jerusalem was not built on the flat plains but among mountains. Just as it could rest and find protection in its geography, so can we rest in God's sovereignty. The Lord surrounds your life with protection, and He always will. As the mountains stand like a fortress around Jerusalem, the Lord surrounds His people with His presence and power.

God's presence is constant, personal, and powerful. He doesn't leave us to face life's dangers alone. Enemies may rise up, storms may rage, but God always encircles us with His loving arms. God's presence surrounds you completely. When the enemy attacks you from behind, God is there. When trouble meets you head-on, God is there. When fear rises from the side, God is there. The psalmist added a phrase that should never be overlooked. He said God's protection is "from this time forth and forevermore." It is not temporary, it doesn't come and go, it doesn't expire. No, God's protection is eternal.

There will never be a moment when God withdraws His surrounding presence. Enemies may change, circumstances may shift, but God's protection always remains. Paul said in Rom. 8:38,39 that nothing "shall separate us from the love of God which is in Christ Jesus our Lord." That's forever protection and eternal security. That is the love of God.

| 15 |

"DESPERATE MEASURES"

The story of the Syrian army's attempt to take the life of Elisha doesn't end with his servant being given vertical vision to see the horses and chariots of fire all around Elisha. The Syrian army came rolling down those hills like a powerful tsunami and Elisha was ready for them. He prayed to the Lord and said, "Strike these people, I pray, with blindness" (2 Kings 6:18). Elisha was surrounded but not afraid because he knew the armies of heaven were with him. God moved and "struck them with blindness according to the word of Elisha" (vs. 18). One moment prior to this Elisha prayed for one man's eyes to be opened and now he prays for eyes of thousands of men to be closed. Miraculously, God answered both prayers. This shows us the power of prayer. James 5:16 says, "The effective, fervent prayer of a righteous man avails much." It can open one man's eyes and close the eyes of thousands.

Elisha has a weapon greater than bows and arrows. He has prayer. No matter who or what you pray about, God will honor that prayer as long as it is in accordance with His will. God's deliverance didn't come through Israel's sword but through His Spirit. You don't fight in the flesh when surrounded by the enemy because God's spiritual weapons are far stronger. 2 Cor. 10:4 says, "For the weapons of our warfare are not carnal but mighty in God for pulling down strongholds." Prayer, faith, and obedience open the door for divine intervention. God answered Elisha's prayer immediately. In the blink of an eye soldiers who thought they were strong and invincible are now blind and helpless, not knowing what to do. When the trials of life surround you, remember that God can disarm the enemy without you lifting a finger. For sure, prayer is stronger than panic and faith is stronger than fear.

The leaders of the Syrian army thought they had the perfect plan to capture Elisha, but the moment God intervened their wisdom became foolishness and their strength became weakness. The enemy may plot and scheme against God's people, but God can overturn human plans in a moment. Is. 54:17 assures us that "no weapon formed against us shall prosper." Watch what happens next. "Now Elisha said to them, 'This is not the way, nor is this the city. Follow me, and I will bring you to the man whom you seek.' But he led them to Samaria" (vs. 19). This is the same thing God says to us when we're lost in confusion. He says, "This is not the way. Follow Me." He never asks us to walk by sight; He calls us to walk by faith (2 Cor. 5:7). In times of confusion let God's Word be your compass. Ps. 119:105 says, "Your word is a lamp to my feet and a light to my path." You may not see the whole picture, but obedience leads to God's perfect will.

God can take what the enemy intends for evil and turn it around for good (Gen. 50:20). Trust God's sovereignty. What looks like defeat may actually be God leading you to victory. Elisha didn't panic and he didn't run away. He simply believed God was in control and trusted Him to turn the situation around. He then led these blinded soldiers to Samaria. Why Samaria? It was the headquarters of the Israelite army and was where the king of Israel was at. They didn't know it but Elisha was leading them step-by-step into God's plan. "As soon as they entered Samaria, Elisha said, 'Lord, open the eyes of these men that they may see.' So the Lord opened their eyes, and they saw they were in Samaria" (vs. 20). Once again we see Elisha's dependence on prayer and God's willingness to act beyond human ability. First he prayed for blindness and then he prayed for sight. His prayers brought forth both protection and revelation.

Imagine the shock of the king of Israel at this turn of events. His enemies are standing before him and they are helpless, vulnerable, at risk, and completely at his mercy. The normal impulse at a time like this is to strike back when the tables turn in our favor. When wronged, betrayed, or attacked, our instinct is to take advantage of the situation at hand. "Now when the king of Israel saw them, he said to Elisha, 'My father, shall I kill them? Shall I kill them?'" (vs. 21). It was a question of instinct. Should he destroy his enemies while he had the chance? What does the Bible say? Prov. 24:17, "Do not rejoice when your enemy falls, and do not let your heart be glad when he stumbles." Yet so often our flesh wants exactly that. The king repeats his question - "Shall I kill them? Shall I kill them? - as if his eagerness betrays his desire for revenge. Clearly, he knows not what to do and therein lies the problem.

To his credit he respects the man of God by calling him "my father," a term of endearment and honor. The king was out for blood and surely didn't expect the response he got. "And he answered, 'You shall not kill them. Would you kill those whom you have taken captive with your sword and your bow? Set food and water before them, that they may eat and drink and go to their master" (vs. 22). One is reminded of Rom. 12:21 that says, "Do not be overcome by evil, but overcome evil with good." The greatest weapon against evil is not vengeance but goodness, not hatred but love. The real test of faith is not how you treat your friends but how you treat your enemies. Can you forgive those who have wounded you? Can you bless those who have cursed you? Think of the cross. God could have destroyed us because of our sin but instead gave us His Son. On the cross Jesus prayed, "Father, forgive them." Through His mercy we are now friends of God.

"So he prepared for them a great feast, and when they had eaten and drunk, he sent them away, and they went to their master. And the Syrians did not come again on raids into the land of Israel" (vs. 23). This single verse teaches us how the kingdom of God operates for it captures the transforming power of grace, a grace that helps and feeds enemies instead of killing them. The real miracle is not that their natural eyes were closed and then opened but that their spiritual eyes were opened to the mercy and compassion of the God Elisha served. The king of Israel wanted to kill the captured Syrians, but grace always interrupts vengeance. Jesus said in Matt. 5:44, "Love your enemies and pray for those who persecute you." Grace isn't natural, it's supernatural. It is not weakness; it is strength under control. The flesh demands payback, but the Spirit calls us to forgiveness. That is the grace of God.

Notice that it was a great feast that was prepared for this army. The food they ate was not a minimal ration of just bread and water. No, they received a banquet prepared just for them. Prov. 25:21,22, "If your enemy is hungry, give him bread to eat. And if he's thirsty, give him water to drink for you will heap burning coals on his head, and the Lord will reward you." This verse teaches us that if you really want to leave a lasting impression on your enemies, be strategic in your kindness to them. Go out of your way and respond to them in love. Don't think not retaliating is all you need to do. No, go a step further and bless, encourage, feed, and help those who did you wrong. Prepare a banqueting table for them to eat at. This feast of forgiveness brought peace between these two nations. No treaty was signed, no army was strengthened, no walls were built higher. Peace came because grace disarmed hostility.

As had happened throughout the Old Testament, the northern kingdom of Israel had turned its back on God. They were worshipping idols, ignoring the prophets, and living in rebellion. Sin had opened the door to judgment. Israel's repeated rebellion against God left them vulnerable. Because of their sin, God allowed the king of Syria to besiege the capital city of Samaria. 2 Kings 6:24,25 says, "Sometime later, however, King Ben-Hadad of Syria gathered his entire army and besieged

Samaria. As a result, there was a great famine in the city." At first glance this event seems contradictory to what was said in the previous verse. Vs. 23 says Syria stopped raiding Israel but the very next verse says Syria attacked again. Look carefully and you will see that vs. 23 says Syria no longer attacked Israel will small bands of raiding parties making quick and brief invasions into the land.

Vs. 24 describes a full-scale military campaign led by the king himself. This didn't happen immediately after the ceasefire in vs. 23 but perhaps months or even years later. Elisha's mercy and kind treatment of the original raiders halted the ongoing cycle of small raids. It brought a temporary lull of hostilities, but political tensions remained. Later, when circumstances changed, the king of Syria launched a massive invasion against Samaria. This is no contradiction, just a shift from one stage of conflict to another. The siege against Israel cut off all supplies and no food could enter the city. The famine became so severe that prices skyrocketed. Surely, death is at the door. This is not simply a story of a famine. It is a spiritual wake-up call. Sin, rebellion, and unbelief always lead to destruction. When God is shut out, the enemy closes in.

Before starvation there is inflation. Vs. 25, "The siege lasted so long that a donkey's head sold for eighty pieces of silver, and a cup of dove's dung sold for five pieces of silver." This verse describes the extreme conditions of the famine and the desperate measures taken by the people to survive. The price of these items reflects the high cost due to the scarcity of food. Eating an unclean donkey's head and the droppings of a dove was not a normal thing to do. But the situation was so bad the people not only ate these things but paid dearly for them. The mention of these animals serves to underscore the extreme deprivation and the lengths to which people were driven to survive in the face of overwhelming adversity. The desperation of the people was everywhere as they struggled with the dire circumstances of the siege. So extreme was this famine that some turned to cannibalism to survive.

Two desperate mothers, driven by unimaginable hunger, made a gruesome pact to boil and eat their own children. They would eat one woman's son and the next woman's son the following day. This horrifying agreement shows how far sin and desperation can drive people when God is not in their lives. Without God society descends into extreme chaos and moral collapse. Hopelessness without faith in God breeds despair. When people reject God's law, they eventually devour one another spiritually, emotionally, and even physically. The first woman boiled her son, and the two women ate him. The next day, the woman who suggested this atrocity hid her son and refused to fulfill her end of the agreement. This angered the first woman, and she went and told the king of Israel what happened in hopes that justice would be served. The king is heartbroken, and it brings him to his breaking point.

The deadly rise of selfishness and self-preservation will surely happen when a culture abandons God. When people reject the truth long enough the unthinkable becomes possible. None of this should have come as a surprise because God warned His people before they entered the Promised Land that things like this would happen if they rejected Him and became disobedient. Deut. 28:52 says enemy armies "shall besiege you in all your towns until your high and fortified walls came down." The longer the people persisted in sin, the more dramatic the consequences would be. Vs. 53, "And you shall eat the fruit of your womb, the flesh of your sons and daughters, whom the Lord your God has given you in the siege and in the distress which your enemies shall distress you." Vs. 54,55 says the most tenderhearted man will eat and devour the flesh of one of his children and refuse to share the child with his own brother, his beloved wife, and his surviving children.

If you think this is bad, it gets worse. Vs. 56,57 says the most tender woman will hide from her husband and children the afterbirth and new baby she has borne so that she can secretly eat them. Later, when the Babylonians besieged Jerusalem, Jeremiah wrote in Lam. 4:10, "The hands of compassionate women have boiled their own children; they became their food during the destruction of the daughter of my people." These are gruesome passages of scripture, but the Lord is warning the people what would happen if they turned their backs on Him. This is horrific, atrocious, and unimaginable. The wages of sin usually are. The consequence of sin brings about the abandonment of natural affections for those we love and, beyond that, the emergence of inhumane behavior where people act like wild beasts. People who were once considered civilized and normal are now animalistic in their compulsions, desires, and pursuits. This is the condition of Samaria that the king of Israel finds himself in.

The king was overwhelmed by the anguish of his people and the unspeakable horrors of the famine. When he heard the words of this woman, he tore his royal robe in grief (vs. 30). "The people looked, and behold, he had sackcloth beneath on his body" (vs. 30). Sackcloth was a rough garment made of goat's hair symbolizing mourning and supposed repentance. Notice that this piece of sackcloth was hidden under his royal robe. Outwardly he appeared as a king of the people but inwardly he was secretly wrestling with guilt and fear. Here is a man who smiles in public but cries in private. He wears the robe of success to hide the scars of a defiant heart. This is a picture of outward religion and inward rebellion. God wants to do something about this situation. He wants to help and rescue the people. At the same time, the evil one likes to create mindsets in people that will block their breakthrough.

One of the main mindsets he uses is blame. The king said in vs. 31, "God do so to me and more also if the head of Elisha the son of Shaphat remains on his shoulders this very day." Desperation without faith leads to rage. Instead of falling on his knees before God, he clinches his fists in anger. His heart is now exposed. He wears sackcloth but plans murder. In his despair, the king contemplates drastic action, seeking to hold Elisha responsible for the city's plight. Instead of turning to God, he wrongfully blames the man of God. The king is not walking with God nor is he seeking God. His rebellion is giving him an evil mindset that doesn't make any sense. Instead of seeking mercy, he seeks a scapegoat. He blames God and the prophet of God for what is happening to the city. Why did he do that? Because it is easier to pass the blame on God and others than it is to look in the mirror.

There is nothing more contradictory than this. While wearing a torn robe and sackcloth underneath, the king plans to kill Elisha, the anointed prophet of God. This is pure hypocrisy. Interesting enough, these are the same words his mother Jezebel said concerning Elijah. She vowed to have Elijah put to death in 1 Kings 19:2 and here Jehoram is saying the same thing about Elisha. While the city trembles and the king fumes, vs. 33 says, "But Elisha was sitting in his house, and the elders were sitting with him." Can you see the contrast here? Outside there is hunger, panic, and chaos while inside there are peaceful and steady hearts. Is. 26:3 says, "You will keep him in perfect peace whose mind is stayed on You, because he trusts in You." Elisha is not just calm; he is discerning as well. The king sent a messenger ahead of him and before he even arrives where the prophet is at God reveals to Elisha the king's murderous plans.

Elisha said to the elders, "Do you see how this son of a murderer has sent someone to take away my head?" (vs. 32). God gave him divine revelation, and he knows exactly what's coming. Finally, the king himself arrives and listen to what he says, "Surely this calamity is from the Lord; why should I wait any longer?" (vs. 33). He is saying God allowed this so why wait and pray? He acknowledges God's sovereignty but instead of trusting God's character he uses God's power as an excuse to give up. He blames God for allowing the famine and decides to stop waiting on Him. This is fatalism, a crisis of faith. Heb. 6:12 says it is through faith and patience that we inherit the promises of God. Real faith is trusting God's heart when you can't see His hand. The reality of life is that it is always darkest just before the dawn. God's delays are not His denials. Little did the king know that deliverance from the famine would come the very next day.

| 16 |

"NOTHING TO LOSE"

A severe famine has ravished the city of Samaria, and it brings forth the depths of suffering, the consequences of desperation, and the balance between faith and despair in the midst of a crisis. Life has moments when the darkness feels unshakable, when the problems we face seem to have the final word. It's into this bleak reality that a word of hope is given by Elisha. Then Elisha said, "Hear the word of the Lord. Thus says the Lord, 'Tomorrow about this time a measure of flour will cost only one piece of silver, and two measures of barley will cost only one piece of silver'" (2 Kings 7:1). In the face of blame and threats, Elisha refuses to stop speaking in faith. He gave the king a staggering promise. In twenty-four hours, God will turn this famine into great abundance. This prophecy sounded absurd. The people were starving and an enemy army surrounded their city. There was no logical pathway for relief yet Elisha declared, "Hear the word of the Lord."

God specializes in impossible situations and His promises are not weakened by famine, siege, or scarcity. He always "calls things that are not as though they were" (Rom. 4:17). Here in Samaria, through Elisha God is speaking light into darkness just as He did at creation. When God speaks, darkness must flee and famine must bow to His word. In the Bible, it is amazing how so often man's evil is met by God's grace. The king of Israel wants to execute the prophet of God and in return God says the famine will end the next day. Consider Rom. 5:8, "While we were yet sinners, Christ died for us." That's the grace of God. When we were His enemies, the Lord reached down and embraced us with His love and grace. We learn here that God's grace can change any circumstance in any amount of time. Within a few hours the people will go from eating the head of a donkey and dove's dung to eating fine flour and barley.

As we shall see, not only does the devil use the mindset of blame to hinder your breakthrough, he also uses the mindset of doubt and unbelief to stop you from receiving your deliverance. Doubt blinds you to the power of God. Vs. 2, "So an officer on whose hand the king leaned answered the man of God and said, 'That couldn't happen even if the Lord opened the windows of heaven.'" The right-hand man of the king didn't react with gratitude but with scorn and unbelief. Saying God can't do something is one of the most evil and foolish things a person could ever say. James 1:16 says the doubter "is like a wave of the sea, driven and tossed by the wind." We must choose to trust God even when logic says it's impossible. Faith doesn't ignore reality, it believes God's reality is greater. The most dangerous type of unbelief is to doubt the goodness of

God. Elisha responds to this man, "You will see it happen with your own eyes, but you won't be able to eat any of it" (vs. 2).

Elisha's declaration of grace turns into a declaration of judgment. This man's hardened heart and skeptical mind would prevent him from partaking of the miraculous provision of God. Anyone who chooses unbelief makes no room for the miraculous power of God. Doubt always blocks the blessings of God because He never responds to unbelief; He only responds to faith. Unbelief questions God's ability and faithfulness and causes you to hesitate instead of obeying. Break the barrier of unbelief and you'll see the blessings of God flow freely in your life. God's desire is to pour out favor, provision, and guidance but when you allow doubt to take root inside of you it short-circuits the power of God and His Word in your circumstances. The children of Israel saw this firsthand. An entire generation missed the Promised Land because they refused to trust God's promise (Heb. 3:19). Their unbelief turned a journey of days into a wilderness of decades.

When Elisha told the king the famine was going to end the next day, he didn't tell him how it was going to happen, how God will use the least likely people to bring about their deliverance. Vs. 3, "Now there were four leprous men at the entrance of the gate and they said to one another, 'Why are we sitting here waiting to die?'" This is a very reasonable question to ask. These lepers were outcasts. They were physically diseased, socially rejected, and economically destitute. They were caught between a starving city behind them and an enemy army before them. These four societal castaways now have an important decision to make. Vs. 4 says, "We will starve if we stay here, but with the famine in the city, we will starve if we go back." With nothing to lose, they said, "So we might as well go out and surrender to the Syrian army. If they let us live, so much the better. But if they kill us, we would have died anyway."

The lepers reasoned among themselves. Staying where they were meant certain death as did going back to the city. But moving forward meant possible death but also the possibility of life. This was the only option that made sense. Faith is choosing the one option that gives God room to work. Faith doesn't deny the risk; it simply believes God is greater than the risk. They didn't know it at the time, but God was prompting them to do this not realizing they would be the means through which Samaria would receive its deliverance from the famine. Of all the people God could have used, He chose the most despised men in their society to accomplish His will. 1 Cor. 1:27 (TPT), "God chose the puny and powerless to shame the high and mighty." If God is willing to recruit lonely, rejected, and diseased individuals who were cut off from any meaningful interactions with other people, how much more can He use you?

Amidst the prevailing despair, vs. 5 says, "And they rose at twilight to go to the camp of the Syrians" (vs. 5). This was the darkest time of night when visibility was at a minimum. These four lepers, men who rely on the scraps on the dump outside the city to survive, are totally unaware that their course of action is going to play into a massive deliverance. There was no supernatural revelation given, no indication that the Lord spoke to these lepers telling them what to do. These were just four men thinking logically about their current situation. What we do know is that God uses those who make the most of the opportunities they've been given. They are choosing the best possible outcome for the limited situation they are in. In like manner, God will honor you if you'll make the best out of what seems to be situations outside of your control. But for that to happen, you must rise up and go forward.

Breakthrough begins when you take a step of faith. These four lepers didn't know what awaited them at the enemy camp. They just knew they had to do something, so off they went. They didn't wait for the sun to rise but acted in the dark. Faith moves when it doesn't see the outcome. Trust God and start moving knowing He meets you on the way, not while you sit still. Instead of waiting for death, these men chose to step into the unknown. "And when they had come to the outskirts of the Syrian camp, to their surprise no one was there" (vs. 5). Unknown to them, God was working behind the scenes. "For the Lord had caused the army of the Syrians to hear the noise of chariots and the noise of horses, the sound of a great army" (vs. 6). This shows us the unseen power of God working on behalf of His people. He didn't need an army to fight this battle; He simply caused the enemy to hear the illusion of a sound that wasn't there.

God's divine intervention manifests in a manner that surpasses human understanding. He always works in unseen ways. While we worry about the battle, He is already arranging the outcome. The Syrians had the upper hand militarily but one move from God changed everything. The people of Samaria couldn't see what God was doing but deliverance was in motion while they were in despair. The Syrians heard phantom armies, so they said to one another, "Look, the king of Israel has hired against us the kings of the Hittites and the kings of Egypt to come against us" (vs. 6). In 2 Kings 6:17 God opened the eyes of Elisha's servant to see the angelic army in the heavenlies. But here He opened the ears of the Syrian army to hear the sound of horses and chariots. Is it possible what the Syrians heard was the same angelic army the servant saw? Was this the sound of the celestial army that surrounded Elisha when the Syrians came to kill him?

So afraid was the Syrian army "they arose and fled at twilight and abandoned their tents, their horses, and their donkeys, leaving the camp as it was, and fled for their lives" (vs. 7). While the lepers were stepping forward, God was already sending confusion into the enemy's camp. This sound struck fear into their souls, and they fled in terror leaving everything behind. God specializes in sudden turnarounds. What looks impossible can become possible in a single moment. Your breakthrough doesn't have to take years; it can happen in the blink of an eye. Don't despair when you're surrounded by the enemy. God has a plan already in motion so trust His timing. Your breakthrough may come in the twilight, when things look darkest. Whatever you're facing today, God can suddenly turn it around. Trust Him and hold on to your faith. In the twilight of your trial God will move and the enemy will surely flee.

"When the men with leprosy arrived at the edge of the camp, they went into one tent after another, eating and drinking wine; and they carried off silver and gold and clothing and hid it" (vs. 8). These lepers, these outcasts of society, walked into the camp and discovered God's miraculous provision. What seemed like their darkest hour turned into a day of unexpected abundance. The very place of their fear became the place of their fulfillment. What was once the enemy's possession became their provision. They entered another tent and hid the spoil from there also (vs. 8). The lepers helped themselves to the bounty they stumbled upon but soon conviction struck their hearts. What they were doing left a bitter taste in their mouths, and they knew something had to be done. "Finally, they said to each other, 'This is not right. This is a day of good news, and we are not sharing it with anyone! If we wait until morning some calamity will certainly fall upon us'" (vs. 9).

We need to have the same conviction these lepers had. The world needs what we have received from the Lord and to keep these blessings to ourselves would be selfish and wrong. Don't hide what God has given you. Share His blessing. Share His Word. Share His love. What He has graciously placed into your hands is to be shared unequivocally with others. Blessings are not to be hoarded. The lepers then said, "'Come on, let's go back and tell the people at the palace.' So they went back to the city and told the gatekeepers what had happened" (vs. 9). Even though God brought about a miraculous deliverance for the people and their situation, it still required somebody to go to them and share the good news about what happened. God has sent each of us into the world to be messengers of hope and not hoarders of blessings. In the heart of every believer should be the readiness to share with others all that He has done.

The lepers openly acknowledged that if they didn't tell others what the Lord had done then some calamity would come upon them. God would hold them accountable for their silence. Paul said in 1 Cor. 9:16, "Woe is me if I don't preach the gospel." He knew withholding the gospel would bring judgment upon himself. The BBE says, "A curse is on me if I do not." To their credit, they did not keep silent. They reported what happened to the gatekeepers who in turn "called out, and they told it to the king's household inside'" (vs. 11). The king arose in the night and when he heard the news of what happened he didn't rejoice but instead thought this was a trap by the enemy to lure them out of the city so they could get in (vs. 12). The world we live in is full of uncertainty, fear, distrust, and skepticism. Many times, when God opens a door of blessing, we hesitate suspecting that it's too good to be true.

The king didn't thank God for this great deliverance but suspected a trap. Instead of believing the word of God spoken through Elisha, he trusted in his own reasoning. The king heard in person Elisha's prophecy, it came to pass, and he still denied it. He was determined to explain away the miracle. He was devout in his skepticism, unwavering in his unbelief. It is wrong and sometimes deadly to have a fatalistic trust in mere human wisdom. This is why Prov. 3:5 says, "Trust in the Lord with all your heart and lean not on your own understanding." The king's heart was blinded to the goodness of God. He had a critical spirit and was devoted to his conspiracy theo-

ries. Why not just trust God and partake of His abundant blessings? The famine was real but so was the deliverance. When
God says He will provide, don't let fear of the unknown make
you suspicious. His ways may surprise us, but they never fail
us.

Fortunately, one of the king's servants had more sense than he
did. With simple, profound logic he said to the king, "We had
better send out scouts to check into this" (vs. 13). This servant's
words came when the city was on the brink of destruction. He
was saying, "We are dying anyway. Why not try? Why not step
out and see if God's word is true?" In the middle of all this despair, this unnamed servant then said, "If something happens
to them, it will be no worse than if they stay here and die with
the rest of us" (vs. 13). God's promises are not to be debated;
they are to be acted upon. This simple suggestion to step out
and act on the word of the Lord became the turning point for
an entire nation. Action had to be taken. They had to step out
beyond the city walls and look for themselves. "So they took
two horsemen, and the king sent them after the army of the
Syrians, saying, 'Go and see'" (vs. 14).

Faith is not passive. It moves; it goes to see. Faith requires you
to walk according to what God has spoken even if you're un-
sure of the outcome. Sometimes, your miracle is one step beyond your fear. More times than not, the battle you're dreading
has already been won. The enemy has fled and all you have to
do is go and see. That's what walking in faith is all about. What
God has promised, He has already performed. Don't let doubt
and fear keep you trapped in your trial when victory is waiting

just outside the gate. Step out and see what God has already done for you. "So they went after them as far as the Jordan, and indeed, all the road was littered with garments and weapons that the Syrians had thrown away in their haste" (vs. 15). What a sight that must have been. Not only did they get food, they got clothes and weapons as well proving that God always does "exceedingly abundantly above all that we ask or think" (Eph. 3:20).

Spread out in front of these scouts was the goodness of God. This was undeniable evidence that God's promise had come true. The king and all the doubters could no longer deny what God had done. When God fulfills His word in your life, He leaves evidence so others will see and know that it was only Him who delivered you. Your testimony is the evidence for others to witness. "So the messengers returned and told the king. Then the people went out and plundered the tents of the Syrians" (vs. 16). God didn't just end the famine; He reversed the economy overnight. Look what happens next. "So a measure of flour was sold for one piece of silver, and two measures of barley was sold for one piece of silver" (vs. 16). Elisha's prophecy had come true. Not only was food available, it was affordable. This, however, was not the only prophecy fulfilled this day. Earlier in the chapter the king's right-hand man mocked what Elisha had predicted.

Elisha responded that the man would see the miracle but not eat of it. Vs. 17, "Now the king had appointed the officer on whose hand he leaned to have charge of the gate. But the people trampled him in the gate, and he died, just as the man of

God had said, who spoke when the king came down to him."
This is a vivid reminder that God's word never fails. Unbelief is always an insult to God's integrity. This sobering passage warns us about the dangers of doubting God but also
encourages us that when God speaks, His word will surely
come to pass. His word is not dependent on circumstances; it
creates new circumstances. Don't measure His promise by the
size of your problem, measure your problem by the size of your
God. Don't stand at the gate of your miracle, doubting what
God has promised. If you walk in unbelief, you may see others receive the blessings of God while you'll be on the outside
looking in.

| 17 |

"RIGHT ON TIME"

Restoration is one of the most beautiful words in the Christian vocabulary. It speaks of something broken being made whole again, something lost being returned, something stolen being restored. 2 Kings 8:1-6 tells of a woman whose life testifies that God not only protects and sustains His people through seasons of famine and lost but also restores abundantly in His perfect timing. This passage continues the story of the Shunammite woman who had showed kindness to Elisha, the same woman who had experienced God's power when her dead son was brought back to life. Now she faces another test of faith but in it we'll see the hand of God who restores beyond measure. He graciously sent Elisha to this woman to prepare her for what was about to happen. He said, "Arise, and depart with your household, and sojourn wherever you can, for the Lord has called for a famine, and it will come upon the land for seven years" (vs. 1).

Before the famine struck, the Lord gave her a word of warning through the prophet. God always prepares His people for trials.

He may not give us all the details, but He never leaves us blindsided. Notice it was God who orchestrated this famine. This reminds us that famines were not natural occurrences under the Old Covenant but were brought about by the people's disobedience. This famine was twice as long as the one that took place during the time of Elijah (1 Kings 17,18). Why? Because the people refused to repent and returned to their sin in a persistent manner. They didn't learn the first time, so God doubled this famine to seven years. To sin willfully after you vowed not to only invites greater discipline from a holy and righteous God. The problem is many people unfortunately deceive themselves by thinking the consequences they had to endure before will be the same and not worse if they indulge in the same sins again.

What specifically did the people do that brought about this famine? The text doesn't say exactly but a key may be found in the opening verse that says, "Then Elisha spoke to the woman..." The word "then" denotes sequence. Something happened before this chapter began and was the reason for Elisha telling the woman that a famine was coming. So, what was it that happened? 2 Kings 7 tells how the people of Samaris were delivered from a man-made famine caused by the invasion of the Syrian army. The people were starving, and God intervened with supernatural provision. The people were eating to their heart's content, and a careful study of this story reveals a staggering omission of something very important. Nowhere does it say the people responded to what the Lord had done. There was no hint of repentance from the people, no acknowledgment of the goodness of God, and no spoken word of gratitude. Indeed, God takes notice of how we respond to His goodness.

It is quite possible, and most likely, that this prolonged famine came about because of a lack of thanksgiving on the part of the people of Israel. Their silence brought about more discipline. God not only takes note of the wrong people do, He also notices the good His servants do as well. This Shunammite woman was a faithful servant and received a personal visit from Elisha. This is God's way of demonstrating the extent of His reward to those who make the effort to serve Him, to those who sacrificially give toward the advancement of His purposes on earth. In the past, God rewarded this woman for her faithfulness with a son she could not have on her own and now, years later, He rewards her with insight into the future. The reason for Elisha's visit was to make sure she and her household would be preserved from the coming famine. This shows how God takes care of those who take care of His people.

Consider Heb. 6:10, "For God is not unjust. He will not forget how hard you have worked for Him, and how you have shown your love to Him by caring for other believers, as you still do." In a world that often forgets, God remembers. People may overlook your kindness, church members may forget your sacrifices, and those you helped may never say "thank you." But know this, while God will never remember your sins (Heb. 8:12), He will never forget your service to Him. To forget the good done in His name would be an act of injustice. God's very nature is righteousness. He who is perfectly just, perfectly faithful, and perfectly loving takes note of every act of love done for His glory. He is not unrighteous to forget. Your love for God spills over into love for people. Jesus said in Matt. 25:40, "Assuredly, I say to you, inasmuch as you have done it unto the least of these My brethren, you did it to Me."

Your smallest act of kindness is actually an offering to Christ Himself. When you encourage a weary soul, feed the hungry, and pray for the sick, you are ministering unto the Lord. Many begin strong but fade away. This is why faithfulness is the test of true devotion. Gal. 6:9, "And let us not grow weary in weel doing, for in due season you will reap if you faint not." God honors continued faithfulness. It's not what you used to do for God that matters most, it's what you're still doing. So keep ministering, keep loving, keep serving. God will not forget. And because God in not unjust, He will repay every act done in faith. For sure, heaven keeps perfect records. Matt. 6:11, "You Father who sees in secret will Himself reward you openly." Nothing done in His name is ever wasted. A cup of cold water given in His name, a prayer whispered in secret, a word of encouragement spoken in love. All of it will yield an eternal reward.

The Shunammite woman had served Elisha faithfully and God did not forget her labor of love. He spoke to the prophet and told him to tell the woman to flee because a famine was coming. God is watching over her, taking care of her, providing for her. Through Elisha God is giving her supernatural revelation of what's about to happen. Not even the king received such a privileged word. Also, an intense, practical truth is found in the instructions Elisha gave her. He told her to leave and sojourn "wherever you can." In other words, he gave her the liberty to choose where to go. Don't be like those people who are troubled by the belief that every decision they make in this life, either big or small, must not be made unless it is approved by supernatural disclosure. Don't remain completely inactive until some spectacular sign is granted to you. This is not only unscriptural but can be very harmful. People who do this live tormented lives.

God has placed in each of us the ability to think, reason, and plan. It is not wrong to dream or to strategize. Prov. 16:9 says, "A man's heart plans his way, but the Lord directs his steps." The truth be told, more times than not God's guidance comes after you've first made some plans. God gave you a brain and He expects you to use it wisely and sensibly. Do the best you can always doing what you think is best. As you plan with your mind, be sure to also pray with your heart. Go to God and say, "Lord, not my will, but Your will be done." Give God the right to redirect your steps. Solomon reminds us that even our best plans are limited. Prov. 14:12, "There is a way which seems right to a man, but its end is the way of death." God's direction can come through circumstances, closed doors, or unexpected turns. But every divine redirection carries divine purpose. What feels like a disruption is really a divine detour.

2 Kings 8:2 says, "So the woman arose and did according to the saying of the man of God, and she went with her household and sojourned in the land of the Philistines for seven years." At this time, the land of Israel was experiencing a season of plenty. The economy was thriving and just when things were going

well, the woman is told to leave for several years. All this woman had to go on was the word from the prophet. With her own eyes she saw the good fortune of those around her and now she's told things would change very quickly. She also was living in comfort. She had land, servants, and stability when suddenly there came a word from the Lord through Elisha that would uproot everything she know. God's word to us sometimes interrupts our plans. It may call us away from what is familiar. It may unsettle what we've built. Yet that is often how God protects us.

This woman's response was commendable. She did not argue or try to reason with the man of God. There was no resistance or protest. Instead, she obeyed in faith and without delay. If the woman had stayed where she was, she would have suffered with the rest of the land. Obedience may have cost her some comfort but it's what opened the door to preservation. There is no record of her asking why. She didn't say, "How will I survive?" or "Where should I go?" The instruction was open-ended. Elisha wasn't specific but she obeyed anyway. Faith doesn't need all the details. Faith moves when God speaks even when it doesn't see the whole picture. Faith may not know what the future holds but it knows Who holds the future. The Shunammite woman didn't know what would happen in those seven years or if the land would still be hers when she returned. She did know that not leaving would be disobedience.

Notice also that this woman left right away. When God speaks, move quickly. Delay in obedience is often disobedience in disguise. Don't wait for understanding, walk in faith and trust. We also know that God sustained her as she sojourned in enemy territory. When God directs your path, He takes responsibility for your provision. Where God guides, God provides. God never forsakes the righteous. David said in Ps. 37:25, "I have been young, and now am old; Yet I have not seen the righteous forsaken, nor his descendants begging bread." This is not just an observation; it is a testimony. David had lived long enough to look back and see God's faithfulness proven time and time again. He had never seen God abandon His own. David speaks from a lifetime of perspective and with the authority of experience. He wrote, "I will fear no evil for You are with me" (Ps. 23:4). He is saying those who trust in God are never alone.

The word "forsaken" means 'abandoned, deserted, left helpless.' God did not forsake Joseph in prison or Daniel in the lion's den. Neither did He forsake the Shunammite woman. God's provision is seen throughout the Bible. The widow of Zarephath's barrel of meal never failed and the manna in the wilderness never stopped until they reached the Promised Land. And let's not forget Phil. 4:19, "But my God shall supply all your need according to His riches in glory by Christ Jesus." Paul is saying God's faithful provision is for those who trust in Him. This is a declaration of divine certainty. Paul had experienced God's faithfulness in abundance and lack, in freedom and captivity. He knew no situation could outmatch God's provision. God always honors the faithfulness of those who walk uprightly. His sovereignty is not proven by the absence of problems, but by His grace and provision in the midst of them.

Vs. 3, "It came to pass, at the end of seven years, that the woman returned from the land of the Philistines; and she went to make an appeal to the king for her house and for her land." This is precise obedience. She calculated her return to her homeland the very moment seven years had passed. She didn't leave a day too soon or a day too late. She left right on time. She obeyed the prophet to the letter and it's this type of obedience that secures God's blessings in your life. It is no wonder this woman was so abundantly blessed throughout her life. She had temporarily lost possession of her property, so she appealed to the king for her house and land. The good news is when you walk with God, nothing you lose is ever truly lost. Obedience does not exempt us from the trials of life. It does, however, guarantee us that God will stand behind His word and make things right for us in His perfect time and place.

She didn't know what would happen when she saw the king, but she went anyway. She took a step of faith not knowing at that very moment God was already arranging her miracle. In the throne room a conversation was taking place. "The king was talking with Gehazi the servant of the man of God, saying, 'Tell me all the great things that Elisha has done'" (vs. 4). This king, like most worldly leaders, had authority, power, and wealth but still he was hungry for something more. This shows there is a void in each of us that only God can fill. The king had heard stories of dead children raised, poisoned stew made better, armies made blind, floating ax heads, and widows provided for. Now he wants to hear it all for himself. So he asks about Elisha, a man who walked with divine power. This reminds us of the power of a testimony about the faithfulness of God and the influence of a servant of God's life.

One is made to wonder how it is that Gehazi had an audience with the king. He was a rebel whose heart had been compromised by greed and deceit, plus he had advanced leprosy. The only explanation is that he had been a servant of Elisha and had seen more miracles than any person in Israel. For this reason, he was called upon to satisfy the king's curiosity. He was granted limited access to the king in order to testify of God's greatness displayed through the prophet Elisha. This shows us that God can use imperfect people to declare His glory. The messenger may be flawed in many ways, but the message is still powerful. Your testimony is the word the world needs to hear. Ps. 107:2 says, "Let the redeemed of the Lord say so." The king asked for a story and Gehazi told it. God instructs all His people to do the same thing, to proclaim His works, to testify of His power, to remind the world God still does great things.

Ps. 145:4 says, "One generation shall praise Your works to another, and shall declare Your mighty acts." Don't let your testimony grow silent. Tell it often and tell it boldly. While Gehazi is testifying about Elisha's miracles, something divine happens. He was telling how Elisha had raised the dead and while he was speaking the evidence walked into the room. "As he was telling the king how he had restored a dead body back to life, that behold, the woman whose son he had restored to life appealed to the king for her house and her land" (vs. 5). This is no coincidence. This is the perfect timing of God. This is a divine appointment showing that God is always working behind the scenes to align people and events for His purpose. "And Gehazi said, 'My lord, O king, this is the woman, and this is her son whom Elisha restored to life'" (vs. 5). When the king saw and heard the woman, there was no denying the power of God.

"And when the king asked the woman, she told him. So the king appointed an official for her, saying, 'Restore all that was hers, and all the proceeds of the fields from the day that she left until now'" (vs. 6). This is a declaration of God's power to bring restoration to not only what was lost, but also what was missed. You may not see it now, but obedience always sets up restoration later. It was this woman's prompt obedience that prepared the way for her restoration to take place. If she had disobeyed and stayed in the land, she might have perished in the famine. But by obeying, by leaving when Elisha told her to go, she lived and God later restored what she lost and multiplied it. We learn from this story that obedience today opens doors tomorrow. Obedience is the visible evidence of faith. It's what brings God's favor, guidance, and reward into our lives. It is one thing to say we trust God, another to show it through our actions.

Abraham obeyed God when told to offer up his son Isaac. Because of his obedience he was abundantly blessed by God. Divine favor not only rested on him but also his descendants. God always attaches blessing to obedience. When we obey, we position ourselves under the umbrella of God's blessings. They may differ in form, but they are always certain. God doesn't restore halfway; He gives back with overflowing abundance. Joel 2:25 says, "I will restore to you the years the locusts has eaten." No enemy can keep what rightfully belongs to you. God used the famine not to destroy the Shunammite woman but to develop her faith. It was in the famine that she learned to trust the word of God more than the comfort of her possessions. And when she returned, she discovered that what she thought was lost was actually being stored up for her return. When you trust God in the famine, He'll meet you in the restoration.

| 18 |

"RESURRECTION POWER"

2 Kings 8-12 tells of the rise and fall of many kings, both in Israel and among their enemies. These chapters trace the turbulent transition of power throughout the land. Prov. 21:1 says, "The king's heart is like a stream of water directed by the Lord; He guides it wherever He pleases." This is a reminder to all of us that God is sovereign over all authorities. Elisha is only mentioned a couple of times in these chapters, but his prophetic influence continues as God raises up and removes kings in order to fulfill His divine will and purpose. 2 Kings 8:7-15 tells how Elisha visits Damascus where Ben-Hadad king of Syria is sick. The king sends his servant Hazael to Elisha to ask if the king would recover. Elisha tells Hazael that the king will recover but that he will die anyway. He then prophesied that Hazael would become king and bring great suffering in the land of Israel. "But it happened on the next day that Hazael took a thick cloth and dipped it in water and spread it over the king's face so that he died, and Hazael reigned in his place" (vs. 15).

In 2 Kings 9 Elisha sends one of the sons of the prophets to anoint the next king of Israel whose name is Jehu. This warrior is tasked with executing judgment on the house of Ahab. Once anointed, Jehu takes immediate action demonstrating the importance of responding promptly to God's call. Our love for God is shown in our obedience to Him without delay. Jehu's mission was not for the faint-hearted. It required boldness and courage. Before long all Baal worship was removed from Israel but there was still one prophesy left to be fulfilled. Years before Elijah had prophesied the death of Jezebel (1 Kings 21:23). Jehu fulfilled this prophesy as Jezebel died a gruesome death being thrown out of a window and eaten by dogs.

As the narrative unfolds, Elisha is not heard from again until 2 Kings 13 when he is at the point of death. Vs. 14 says, "Elisha had become sick with the illness of which he would die." Life is a vapor. People come and go; kingdoms rise and fall. Elisha is at the end of his earthly journey yet even in his weakness he demonstrates the power of a life fully surrendered to God. There is a quiet dignity in this moment. Elisha lies still but his influence and prophetic power remain alive for he knows God is able to show His strength through human frailty. Never mistake physical weakness for spiritual failure. 2 Cor. 12:9 says God's "strength is made perfect in weakness." When you're too weak to stand, you're still strong enough to believe. Elisha had lived an incredible life and in his dying moments Joash the king of Israel comes to him and weeps because he recognizes that Elisha was more than just a mere man.

He said to the prophet, "O my father, my father, the chariots of Israel and their horsemen!" (vs. 14). These are the same words Elisha said when Elijah was taken into heaven (2 Kings 2:12). The king is acknowledging that the strength of Israel was not armies but the prayers and presence of God through the prophet. Yes, Elisha is sick, but the power of God is undiminished. The tears he shed is an indication of his commendable comprehension to the impact Elisha had on the nation. So strong was his admiration for this man that he called him his father. He could not deny Elisha's role in the stability of the people. For sure, this anointed man of God and his walk with the Lord was the true source of the nation's security and strength. Even as the body of Elisha weakens, he still commands the respect of the king. As Joash weeps we are reminded that people with positions of power still depend on people of prayer.

Joash was not a good king for 2 Kings 13:11 says "he did evil in the sight of the Lord." Acknowledging the goodness of God and His people is no indication that one's heart is right with the Lord. Even so, his grief appears to be genuine because in his heart he believes it was Elisha who kept the nation together. As death approaches, Elisha has one final word for this wayward king. The northern kingdom of Israel is in spiritual decline, and the Syrian army is oppressing the people. With all this happening, Elisha now extends comfort to this troubled ruler. Elisha, frail in body but full of the Spirit of God, gives Joash a prophetic sign, telling him to take a bow and some arrows and to put his hand on the bow (vs. 15,16). The king promptly obeyed. Elisha then puts his hands on the king's hands symbolizing God's empowerment. The arrow of victory represents God's promise of deliverance from the desperate times the nation is now in.

Elisha then told the king to open the east window and shoot the arrow (vs. 17). This command was not an old man's ritual but an invitation for the king to participate in God's promise. Faith without works is dead (James 2:17). God gives us promises but He requires faith-filled actions to bring them to life. It is not enough to hear God's word; you must respond to it. God told Joshua, "Every place the sole of your foot shall tread, I have given to you" (Josh. 1;3). The land was promised but Joshua and the people had to fight to possess it. Likewise, Joash had a promise but he had to act in faith to receive it. The arrow he shot represented the will and purpose of God. It was a declaration of victory before the battle began. Elisha said to the king who stood before him, "This is the Lord's arrow, an arrow of victory over Syria, for you will strike the Syrians at Aphek until you have destroyed them" (vs. 17).

Elisha is telling the king he will overcome his enemies. Joash needed to hear this because he's thinking when Elisha dies all hope for victory will die with him. No, people die but God lives forever. The prophet calls the arrow the "arrow of the Lord's deliverance." He's saying the king's source of strength is in God alone. He's telling the king to take his eyes off of him and put them on the Lord above. Ps. 33:20-22, "We put our hope in the Lord. He is our help and our shield. In Him our hearts rejoice, for we trust in His holy name. Let Your mercy be upon us, for our hope is in You alone." Elisha says Joash will have the empowerment to defeat the enemy of the people of God. However, the degree of this victory will be determined by the degree of faith that the king has. The promise of power has been given. It's there for the taking. The question is, how much faith does the king have? A test of obedience is given to reveal his level of expectation.

"And he said, 'Take the arrows,' and he took them. And said to the king of Israel, 'Strike the ground with them," (vs. 18). Notice there are no instructions on how many times to do this. This was a test of the king's heart. Will he strike until Elisha says to stop? Will he strike until every ounce of his strength is gone? Will he strike until the promise felt certain? Instead, "he struck three times, and stopped." Why stop there? Perhaps it felt foolish. Perhaps he didn't see the point. Perhaps he thought it didn't matter. But God was watching. "Then the man of God was angry with him and said, 'You should have struck five or six times; then you would have struck down Syria until you had destroyed it. But now you will strike Syria only three times'" (vs. 19). Five or six times would have meant total victory over Syria. Elisha is saying Joash will now win only a few battles. He'll win enough to survive but not enough to conquer.

The frustration expressed by Elisha reveals his disappointment in the king's limited commitment. The king's failure signified a missed opportunity for complete triumph. Joash showed a lack of spiritual passion. God had provided total victory, but the king's lack of zeal meant only partial deliverance. A divided heart wins only half the battles. Elisha's last prophetic act is meant to teach us one vital truth: God's promises are certain, but our faith determines how fully we experience them, that every act of faith moves the hand of God. When surrounded by your enemies, don't stop praying. Don't stop believing, don't stop obeying, don't stop striking the ground. Let your obedience be relentless. Let your faith be fierce. Keep striking even when your situation looks hopeless, when nothing seems to be working. Believe that every strike of faith matters, that every act of faith shakes the heavens.

If we believe God can do great things, we will obey Him with boldness and persistence. If we doubt, we will obey only part way like Joash and settle for less than God's best. Keep striking until the victory is complete. With Joash what started out as a hopeful moment ended in disappointment. His half-hearted obedience revealed his half-hearted faith. He was willing to go through the motions but was not willing to press through until the promise was complete. He did what Elisha said to do but without strength of purpose and heart. God gives promises but we must move in faith to see them fulfilled. Noah had to build the ark, Abraham had to leave his homeland, and Joshua had to march around the walls. Faith isn't passive; it's active. It doesn't wait for God to move; it moves because God already spoke. Act on what God says. Shoot your arrow, strike the ground, move in faith.

And then the inevitable happened. "So Elisha died, and they buried him" (vs. 20). There was no fanfare, no opened heavens, no chariots of fire, and no whirlwind to take him home. Elisha died a normal death. It seems almost anticlimactic. After all that he accomplished, after decades of ministry and pouring out his life for God, his death is described in a mere seven words. Despite the brevity of this account, Elisha's influence and legacy was profound, as evidenced by the fact that he performed more miracles than anyone else in the Bible, second only to Jesus. The prophet who once raised the dead now lays still. The voice that once thundered with divine authority is now silent. The mantle that once parted rivers is now folded in the tomb. His death is almost startling in its simplicity. The great prophet Elisha, the man who spoke with kings and commanded armies with a word, has now passed on to the other side.

No thunder roared in the sky and no crowds gathered to mourn his passing and to say goodbye. There was only a quiet burial as his body was placed in an unremarkable tomb. Elisha's death left a spiritual void in the land. As his body is laid to rest, vs. 20 adds a dark note, "And the raiding bands from Moab invaded the land in the spring of the year." Right after Elisha died, the enemy came. When he was alive, his prayers had been a covering over Israel. His presence had been a wall of protection around all who lived there. But when that covering was removed, chaos broke loose. The nation Elisha continually prayed for is now under attack. The people now face corruption, fear, and death. Many may think Elisha's story ends here but it doesn't. His death was not the end of his ministry. As we shall see, the anointing on a man of God still has power when the person dies.

Everywhere Elisha went, heaven followed. Every word he spoke carried divine weight. Every miracle pointed to a living God. But now he's gone and Israel has moved on as if nothing happened. What follows is one of the most fascinating, supernatural occurrences in all the Bible. It had not happened before and has not happened since. It is truly a one-of-a-kind miracle. "As a man was being buried, behold, a band of raiders was seen and the man was thrown into the grave of Elisha, and as soon as the man touched the bones of Elisha, he revived and stood on his feet" (vs. 21). Think about that! Elisha has been dead and buried for a while and his body has decayed. His flesh has returned to dust but in his dry bones remained a residue of divine power. The influence of a godly life goes beyond the grave. It's like perfume spilled on the ground but its fragrance remains. Elisha's bones still spoke; they declared God's power and faithfulness.

There are many stories of living men raising the dead but nowhere in recorded history do you hear of a dead man raising another dead man back to life. But it happened here. Elisha died but his influence did not. His bones still spoke, his life still ministered, his God still reigned. If you walk in the Spirit, the power that filled you will remain after you're gone. To understand the power that remained in his bones you must remember that Elisha was no ordinary man. He was a man whose life was marked by the power of God. Since receiving a double portion of Elijah's spirit, he walked in a supernatural dimension of faith and obedience. Every step of his ministry bore the mark of God's divine power. He was a man fully surrendered to God, and because of that, God filled him with power that did not fade away. The power in his life was still present in his death.

The anointing outlasted the man who carried it. Heb. 11:4 says about Abel, "He being dead still speaks." That's what happened here. Elisha's bones preached a sermon without words. Those dry bones became a symbol of hope, healing, and divine intervention. The enduring legacy of Elisha's power even after his death becomes a source of inspiration to all of us. This event was not a random miracle; it was a message from God to His people. Just as there is still power in Elisha's bones, there is still power in what God established long ago. There is still power in the Word of God that was written thousands of years ago. There is still power in the cross of Calvary and the blood of Jesus though it was shed centuries past. There is still power in the Holy Spirit who fell at Pentecost and is still filling believers today. The power that God releases never expires and the anointing never runs out.

The body of the dead man touched the bones of Elisha and came back to life. When you come in contact with the presence of God, dead hearts come alive and dead dreams are revived. You don't have to be perfect. You don't have to understand everything. All you have to do is come in contact with the Spirit of God and the power that raised this man will raise you up also. This miracle symbolizes something greater. It foreshadows the resurrection power of Jesus Christ. Every sinner who comes into contact with Jesus miraculously comes alive. The bones of Elisha gave temporary life, but the body of Jesus that was broken and raised up gives eternal life. Elisha's tomb was opened by accident; the Lord's tomb was opened on purpose. Rom. 8:11 says, "Yes, God raised Jesus to life! And since God's Spirit of Resurrection lives in you, He will also raise your dying body to life by the same Spirit that breathes life into you."

The dust of centuries has long settled over the hills of Israel, yet the story of Elisha continues to breathe into all of us the divine and supernatural power of Almighty God. From the quiet call in the field of Abel Meholah to his death many years later, Elisha's life was a testimony that the Spirit of the Lord is all powerful and not bound by human weakness. His life was not one of comfort, wealth, or worldly acclaim, but of service, obedience, and unwavering faith. He healed the sick, fed the hungry, raised the dead, and turned kings' hearts toward the living God. From the moment Elijah's mantle fell upon his shoulders, Elisha walked in a sacred calling that demanded total surrender, fearless courage, and a steadfast heart anchored in God's promises. His request for a double portion of Elijah's spirit was not a plea for recognition or power but for divine enablement. He desired the strength to carry on the sacred work Elijah began.

Elisha became a vessel through which God's compassion, justice, and power were displayed. Elisha's ministry was not centered on himself, but on showing that the God of Israel was alive, attentive, and merciful to those who trusted Him. He carried on the prophetic mission faithfully, year after year, through shifting kings and changing seasons, always speaking the word of the Lord, even when it was unpopular or dangerous to do so. In the end, Elisha died as he lived - faithful, steadfast, and full of the Spirit of God. Elisha's legacy transcends time because it points to the living presence and power of God that still moves among His people today. Elisha's life reminds us that the call of God is not measured by status, but by surrender; not by fame, but by faithfulness. He teaches us that divine power flows through humble vessels, through those who dare to believe that God can do the impossible. Elisha's ministry closes not with a triumphant parade, but with a quiet assurance: the same God who parted the Jordan, who filled empty vessels with oil, who blinded armies and opened spiritual eyes, still moves today among those who dare to believe.

SUMMARY

The life of Elisha stands as one of the most extraordinary and inspiring stories in all of Scripture—a portrait of unwavering faith, bold obedience, and divine power at work through human surrender. From the moment he was called from the plow to the day the chariots of fire carried his mentor away, Elisha's journey reveals what it means to live wholly yielded to the will of God. His was not a life of comfort or acclaim, but of relentless pursuit after the presence and power of the Almighty.

When the mantle of Elijah fell upon him, Elisha did not merely inherit a prophet's robe—he inherited a mission. His request for a *double portion* of Elijah's spirit was not born of ambition, but of deep spiritual hunger. He longed to do even greater works for the glory of God and the good of His people. That divine hunger became the defining mark of his ministry, setting him apart as a man who believed that God could, and would, do the impossible.

Elisha's story unfolds like a tapestry woven with miracles—each one a thread of faith in action. He healed poisoned waters, multiplied a widow's oil, raised the dead, fed the hungry, and opened blind eyes to see the unseen. Yet behind every miracle lay a simple truth: Elisha trusted God completely. Where others saw impossibility, he saw opportunity for God's power to be revealed. His life teaches us that faith is not merely believing in miracles—it is living in constant expectation of them.

Unlike Elijah, who often thundered from the mountaintop, Elisha's ministry was characterized by compassion, patience, and quiet strength. He was a prophet of presence—walking among kings and commoners alike, bringing divine intervention into ordinary circumstances. His miracles were not merely signs of power; they were expressions of God's care for His people. Through Elisha, we see a God who heals the broken, provides for the needy, and reveals His glory even in the smallest details of life.

Elisha's faith endured through times of turmoil and transition. He lived during a period when Israel's faith was faltering, when idolatry and corruption had taken deep root in the nation. Yet he remained steadfast, unshaken by the darkness around him. He served kings who often ignored his counsel, yet he continued to speak truth with courage and grace. His ministry reminds us that faithfulness is not measured by popularity or visible success, but by perseverance in obedience.

Even in death, Elisha's life testified to the enduring power of God. When his bones revived a dead man who touched them, it was as if God Himself declared that His anointing does not die with the servant—it lives on through the faith of those who continue the work. Elisha's legacy is one of lasting influence, a reminder that those who walk closely with God leave behind a trail of life that others may follow.

Elisha's story invites us to reflect deeply on our own calling. Like him, we are each invited to trade the plow for the prophet's path—to leave behind the familiar and step into the unknown with faith as our guide. His life challenges us to seek a "double portion" of God's Spirit, not for our glory, but that the world may see His hand at work through us. It calls us to live boldly, love deeply, and serve faithfully, trusting that God can use ordinary people to accomplish extraordinary things.

In the end, Elisha's life is not merely the record of a prophet—it is a mirror for every believer who longs to see God move mightily in their generation. His story whispers to us still: *"Where is the Lord God of Elijah?"* And the answer echoes through the ages—He is here, moving through those who, like Elisha, are willing to believe, obey, and never look back.